L'ATELIER
of Joël
ROBUCHON

Designers: Rampazzo et associés
Stylist: Laurence Mouton
Layout and adaptation for English version: ACCORD, Toulouse - France

Van Nostrand Reinhold Staff:
President: Marianne Russell
Vice President, Editorial Design and
Production: Renee Guilmette
Vice President, Marketing and
  Communications: John Muchnicki
Editorial Director: John Boyd
Executive Editor: Pamela Chirls
Editor: Karen Hadley
Marketing Manager: Paula Criscuolo
Support Staff: Michelle Agosta,
  Heather Haselkorn, Kimmee
  Davidson, Carla Nessler

I(T)P® an International Thomson Publishing Company
        The ITP logo is a registered trademark used herein under license

Printed in France

For more information, contact:

Van Nostrand Reinhold
115 Fifth Avenue
New York, NY 10003

Chapman & Hall GmbH
Pappelallee 3
69469 Weinheim
Germany

Chapman & Hall
2-6 Boundary Row
London
SE1 8HN
United Kingdom

International Thomson Publishing Asia
221 Henderson Road #05-10
Henderson Building
Singapore 0315

Thomas Nelson Australia
102 Dodds Street
South Melbourne, 3205
Victoria, Australia

International Thomson Publishing Japan
Hirakawacho Kyowa Building, 3F
2-2-1 Hirakawacho
Chiyoda-ku, 102 Tokyo
Japan

Nelson Canada
1120 Birchmount Road
Scarborough, Ontario
Canada M1K 5G4

International Thomson Editores
Seneca 53
Col. Polanco
11560 Mexico D.F. Mexico

1 2 3 4 5 6 7 8 9 10 FR 03 02 01 00 99 98

Library of Congress Cataloging-in-Publication Data furnished upon request.

Wells, Patricia
  L'Atelier of Joel Robuchon: The artistry of a master chef and his protégés

  ISBN 0-442-02652-8

http://www.vnr.com
product discounts • free email newsletters
software demos • online resources

email: info@vnr.com
A service of I(T)P®

L'ATELIER

of Joël

ROBUCHON

THE ARTISTRY OF A MASTER CHEF AND HIS PROTÉGÉS

TEXT BY PATRICIA WELLS

PHOTOGRAPHS BY HERVÉ AMIARD

Under the direction of Philippe Lamboley

VAN NOSTRAND REINHOLD

I(T)P® A Division of International Thomson Publishing Inc.

New York • Albany • Bonn • Boston • Detroit • London • Madrid • Melbourne
Mexico City • Paris • San Francisco • Singapore • Tokyo • Toronto

S U M

M A R Y

Each historical era has been marked by the skill of certain great chefs. As we near the end of the twentieth century, only a very few can claim such a distinction.

This collection, "The Masters of Gastronomy," enables us to make the acquaintance of those chefs who have created schools of cuisine, imparting their knowledge through veritable *ateliers* and leaving a lasting impact on culinary trends through their technical knowledge and their approach to the palette of products.

Currents of thought are very influential in gastronomy, determining even the choice of produce going into the consumer's shopping basket.

A master cook, with his close circle of pupils, never ceases to investigate new ways of preparing food, of associating tastes and textures. These explorations result in greater refinement and pave the way for an evolution in culinary artistry in all its forms, from the conservation of foodstuffs and the cultivation of the common potato to research into dietetics.

The image of the *Atelier* is strongly present in the taste laboratories which constitute the kitchens of the few great masters of gastronomy. Each dish is an ephemeral work of art, created under the direction and supervision of the chef. The latter is often present at the " pass " to add the finishing touches which represent his trademark

The other chefs and assistants faithfully reproduce the master's recipes in a constant apprenticeship. As in painting, the chef's disciples have to respect certain limits. The most talented set these limits for themselves in order to open up a restaurant in their turn and perhaps free themselves, little by little, from the sway of the master.

This book is divided into three main chapters in order to gain a better understanding of the concept of the *Atelier*, to help decipher its codes and appreciate its many aspects.

The first chapter is presented in narrative style and is illustrated by black and white photographs which bring out the force, and sometimes the suffering, behind this hive of activity. The choice of black and white highlights the often extremely subtle differences of atmosphere, concentration and work at the heart of each *atelier*.

The second chapter, in which color photographs make an appearance, plunges us into the world of the produce essential to the master's creative process. The discovery of this palette of tastes and textures leads us naturally into the third chapter.

In this chapter we admire the skill of the master chef which constitutes the very expression of his knowledge and of the teachings imparted to five of his most talented pupils. It is a veritable technical study based around eight products. The different interpretations shed light on the strengths of the *Atelier*: certain recipes still betray a marked influence of the master whilst others are already moving away and opening up new creative paths. But all carry the hallmark of the school of precision that is Joël Robuchon's.

Philippe Lamboley

The atelier

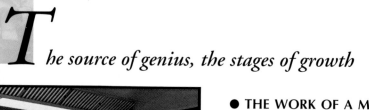

*T*he source of genius, the stages of growth

Today at the youthful age of 51, Joël Robuchon is the food world's most revered creator, leader, mentor, teacher. It is rare that anyone who deals with Robuchon – as student, colleague, food supplier, restaurant client, acquaintance or friend – is not influenced, even in a minute way, by having contact with the master.

● THE WORK OF A MASTER

To describe Joël Robuchon as a cook is a bit like calling Pablo Picasso a painter, Luciano Pavarotti a singer, Frédéric Chopin a pianist. Certainly in each century a master comes along to transform the art form of his choice and Joël Robuchon will undoubtedly go down in history as the artist who most influenced the 20th-century world of cuisine.

To understand the man, one needs to examine the events and the masters that have helped define his philosophy and style, the various periods of his own formation.

One must also understand the man's single-minded mission, to excel and give the best of himself every day.

Like Picasso and the colorful, ever-shifting periods of his life's work, Robuchon's artistic career is ever evolving.

Like Pavarotti's quest for that perfect high C, Robuchon is always in search of a greater purity of taste, finer technique, superiority of freshness, absolute harmony of ingredients and resulting flavors.

"I have never wanted my food to have that big bang that does not endure," he says, likening that style to the forceful sounds of Ravel's "Bolero." Rather, he likens his goals to that which was achieved by Vivaldi in his "Four Seasons."

"You hear the storms but you are not carried away by them. They are all part of the perfect harmony of the sound," he explains.

Following a career that was launched at the age of 15 in a small kitchen in Poitiers in central France, Joël Robuchon was to realize a justly rewarded dream of achieving the top, three-star Michelin rating, at the age of 38. Robuchon now turns a page in gastronomic history to embark upon a new period in his creative life.

After thirty years behind the stove, he leaves behind the daily demands of what has long been considered the best restaurant in the world. But he is far from retiring his toque.

Moving from a period of exclusive, limited influence (where a mere eighty diners a day could partake of his creative genius), Robuchon expands to an era of mass influence, embarking upon a new role as gastronomic ambassador and master teacher (with television shows and hopes for a professional cooking school in Paris) as well as consultant to supermarket chains, hotels and restaurants, and industrial food processors. He intends, as well, to complete a major gastronomic tome designed to replace the aging bible of French cooking, George-Auguste Escoffier's "Le Guide Culinaire."His goals, throughout, have remained the same, and with them he has influenced a generation of chefs who have come under his tutelage.

He has consistently fought for greater attention to technique in cooking, greater understanding of ingredients, and greater insistence on quality in his restaurants.

All the while he preaches his message over and over and over again, which extolls the quality of human work and the satisfaction of a job well done. As if his plate were not already full, Robuchon maintains his love affair with Japan, as he continues to oversee his luxurious gastronomic temple in Tokyo's Château Restaurant Taillevent-Robuchon, a venture he shares with Paris restaurateur, Jean-Claude Vrinat.

Joël Robuchon manages to subtly weave the most complex fare with the simplest, to marry the most commonplace ingredients with the most lofty, pairing "noble" products with those less so.

● THE MAN AT THE TOP

Watching Joël Robuchon at work, and sampling the results of what is produced in his atelier, is akin to examining a flawless, finely-tuned Swiss watch. Technical, yes. But also one of a kind, crafted with years of experience, expertise and care. I doubt that many chefs think as intensely about their food, their work, their direction, as does Robuchon. Nothing happens by accident: it is as though each and every heartbeat is calculated and considered in advance. Yet Joël Robuchon keeps astonishing us all with his ability to reinvent himself moment by moment.

If you hastily examine chef Robuchon's cuisine, you might at first think he's a man gone mad. After all, what sane person would even dream up the idea of sectioning twenty lemons, one by one, to create the world's most puckery lemon tart? Or who, in these cholesterol-crazed days, would consider offering ethereal mashed potatoes that are virtually half butter and half potato? Robuchon is also the man who painstakingly coils strands of spaghetti inside individual savarin molds as a lining, insists that all peppers be peeled, manages to make diners fall on their knees over such unlikely combinations as cauliflower and caviar. His lobster recipe is made up of no less than twenty steps, and that is a serving for two!

But look more closely, more deeply, and you will see that there is method to his madness.

Much of Robuchon's success can be credited to his ability to extract the very essence of an ingredient, creating a very personalized style of cuisine with flavors that are generous, intense and distinctive.

Since he first rose to Michelin three-star fame in 1984, it is three signature dishes – his gelée de caviar, the truffle tart, and potato puree that have become the cornerstone of his reputation – dishes that will no doubt go down in history and be copied (for better and for worse) for decades to come.

Add to those dishes two very simple items: a tossed green salad and homemade bread. Today, one does not think twice about a chef who bakes his own bread. But when Robuchon began serving his tiny sourdough rolls, his walnut-studded bread and fresh toast brushed with garlic, it was downright revolutionary.

His "Salade maraîchère aux truffes" – a heavenly mix of multiple greens and an avalanche of fresh herbs all infused with infinitesimally minced fresh black truffles – has been copied worldwide, and helped bring the simple green salad back to the tables of France's gastronomic temples.

Joël Robuchon allows his cooking to speak for him. Take one bite of his food and you'll see that in his life and his cuisine he is obsessed with perfection, all the while insisting that perfection is an unattainable goal.

Lobster is cooked within a milli-second of perfection and harmonized with a delicate hand of many spices.

A single rouget is filleted, boned, and spread open like a book, set atop grilled slices of garlic and thyme-inf-used potatoes, complemented by a deep-fried basil leaf. With a crunch, a softness, a crispy-tenderness, the flavors explode in your mouth.

● WHY IS HIS FOOD SO DIFFERENT?

Some might complain that the result could be fare that is too intellectual, too studied, not spontaneous. In other chefs' hands, maybe. But not with Robuchon. Each dish seems to be born of looking into the soul of every ingredient and understanding its strengths, its weaknesses. He then molds, melds, seasons and extracts the greatness out of everything from cauliflower to razor clams, to foie gras, to caviar. It's as though there is a combination herb/garden/potager/spice chef all fused together somewhere in the corner of his brain, ready to sprinkle, shower or infuse.

And like any fine artist, his own person-ality is in the end expressed by his work, by what is on the plate. Robuchon brings the palate to heights it never dreamed of.

Some dishes are like a jigsaw puzzle that isn't complete until the last piece is in place: fat, fresh morel mushrooms, crushed foie gras and calf's foot jelly come together to form an etuvée – not a soup, not a main course, so perfect and shimmering you don't want to ruin it with a spoon.

Take the ensemble of recipes presented here: I doubt that anyone has ever thought of , or for that matter, dared combine such uncommonly paired ingredients as lobster and chestnuts in the "Homard aux truffes en cocotte lutée." In cooking, we are always taught that "what grows together goes together." Brittany and the Ardèche are hardly adjacent regions! And one never thinks of them in the same breath. Yet something in his mind and his palate lead him to realize that the nutty, earthy, dense flavor of the chestnut would be happily paired with the iodine-rich, dense meat of the lobster. The addition – lightening one might even say – of fresh basil, a touch of tomato confit, garlic, star anise, bulb fennel and rosemary work together to create an entire symphony of flavors that serve as a backup for the essentially dominant flavors of the lobster and chestnuts.

In his famed "Baby zucchini with bacon, fresh almonds and mint," he again plays with our own curiosity and preconceived notions of what constitutes a normal marriage of flavors. The result is a truly exotic dish, but one that our palate accepts without question. The crunch of the tender baby zucchini pairs perfectly with the crunch of the fresh almond. The nut's sweetness contrasts with the bacon's saltiness, while the brilliant touch of curry serves to unite the zucchini, almond and bacon, bringing them, as it were, into the same surroundings. A final touch of mint serves to wake up the palate, keeping it alert and ready to concentrate on the varied ingredients presented in this single, complex dish.

Joël Robuchon makes the unfamiliar taste familiar once again by pairing wild cèpe mushrooms with eggplant.

In his "Cèpes grillés au thym et caviar d'aubergines," we are served up a combination of croquant and smooth, with the buttery eggplant caviar contrasting sharply with the crunchiness of the slivers of deep-fried eggplant. We approach a double dose of smokiness with the rich smoky flavors of the perfectly grilled mushrooms, and the inherent smokiness of the eggplant caviar.

Robuchon's "Purée de pommes de terre" (Mashed potatoes) is now so famous one would think there was little else to say about it. Yet no other chef has managed to offer a puree as loved or in demand as his pure blend of butter and potatoes.

Years ago, he walked away from the classic potato puree, in which potatoes are first peeled, then simmered in salt water. This method robs the potato not only of much of its earthy flavor, but leaves it devoid of many vitamins contained in its thick, dark, protective skin.

There is no mystery here, only an attempt to render homage to the potato, selecting the freshest and finest and treating it with due respect. With the puree, we can't ignore Robuchon's desire to bring back everyone's memory of childhood flavors. Simplicity and purity – with a trademark Joël Robuchon embellishment – are best displayed in his "Scallops roasted in their shells with herb and butter." Here, the rich, voluptuous and meaty scallop is treated with utmost care and the least complication.

The diner will barely detect the lime zest, the orange juice, anise liqueur or the fresh dill that go into the oven-braised scallops.

The youngest, newest chef in the kitchen is often assigned "potato duty." It is his job to turn out a perfect puree twice each day, whipping and smoothing, blending and tasting, seasoning and perfecting.

And they shouldn't.

The litany of ingredients are there for background, for support, as a way to pay homage to the purity and richness of these giant nuggets from the sea.

The "Truffled sweetbreads with romaine lettuce and herbal cream sauce" is another brilliant combination that rewards the palate with a symphony of flavors assembled from a minimum of ingredients. The star of the show in the end is not the main ingredient – the sweetbread – but rather the avalanche of truffles that stud this rich and tender organ meat. It is that contrast of crunchy truffle with soft sweetbread that lulls the palate into a soothed, satisfied state. The crunchy leaves of romaine serve almost as a

background salad, refreshing with its creamy herbal sauce, one that absorbs the lively flavors of summer savory and tarragon.

After the mashed potatoes – "Purée de pommes de terre," the most classic Robuchon dish presented here – is the "Truffle, onion and bacon tartlets."

I think of this creation as the perfect puzzle, almost a network of dishes combined into one. The truffle seems to be the star here, but in truth it is the complex flavors created by, again, a handful of ingredients that transform what might be a simple dish into one full of elaborate flavors.

The background here is formed by a very basic peasant sauce that combines onions and garlic cooked to a melting tenderness in

The brigade of chefs are like magicians. Their art is created in silence, surrounded by an avalanche of aromas: smoky, steamy vapors and divine scents that bear witness to the chefs' sheer talents.

goose fat, bathed in cream and enhanced by the meaty, salty touch of bacon. (This portion of the dish is simply brilliant all on its own, as a topping for thin slices of toast or as a garnish for roast meat or poultry.)

It is the assembly of the dish – those signature rounds of truffles, layered painstakingly in perfect circles – that separates Robuchon and his chefs from the rest of the culinary world. This precision exists for precision's sake only. Once again, the truffle is treated with incomparable respect: those discs of truffles, so thin, so fine, so elusive, bring out the best of the truffle. The aroma is there, right at the top. The crunch is there, with every bite. As one cuts into the tiny tart, one is both overwhelmed by the power of the truffle and amazed at the comfort with which it seems at home with the soft layer of onion, the thin slip of pastry, the last-minute embellishment of fine sea salt and freshly ground pepper.

● 1945 TO 1960:
THE FORMATIVE YEARS

Joël Robuchon, of course, did not come into the world full-grown and fully formed. He was not an ordinary cook who just woke up lucky one day and was awarded the world's top accolades.

Although his childhood and past do not immediately convince one that his path to the top was straight and direct, in truth there were few detours. His determination to be the best in whatever he did, lead him to where he is today.

Joël Robuchon was born on April 7 1945, in Poitiers, an historic city in central France, roughly halfway between Paris and Bordeaux.

His father was a mason and his mother a housewife. In his youth, his palate, yet unformed, was not unlike that of any modern child. He was what is known as a "picky eater" and his diet was virtually limited to steak and fried potatoes, except on Friday, when his mother served him eggs, and Sunday, when the traditional golden roast

Joël Robuchon created a small, intimate, private dining space adjacent to the kitchen. In this privileged spot, he can survey the kitchen, intervening when something goes wrong. Here, he welcomes one of his mentors, Charles Barrier, who passed on to Robuchon his own passion for the sacred nature of excellent bread made daily.

chicken made its way to the family table.

Like any child of that era living in the country, he had first-hand contact with nature. In the family garden, he helped plant lettuce and escarole, while he learned to pick wild pissenlits from the fields. With school chums, he fished in streams nearby, and with his father, he learned to hunt partridge, pheasant and blackbirds.

At neighboring farms, he watched cider making, picked fresh cherries, and witnessed the annual pig-killing ritual.

The palate of the artist was slowly, unconsciously being formed: "At the time, they may have seemed like little, everyday things," he likes to say now, "but those little things made an impression on me, they brought me close to nature and, most of all, created in me a respect for all living things, a respect for the products of a chef."

At the age of twelve, he entered the seminary. During his seminary years, his quietest, most enjoyable moments were spent helping the nuns in the seminary's kitchens. "Whenever the nuns called for a volunteer to help out in the kitchen, I'd be there," Robuchon recalls.

"They were some of the most relaxing and rewarding moments of my life. Those years in the country helped create a foundation of experience: I know the subtle differences between a fresh shoot of chives and that of an onion. I know the scent of fresh garlic...."

At the age of fifteen, family problems required that he leave the seminary and find employment.

Thus in 1960, he became a youthful apprentice at the hôtel-restaurant Relais de Poitiers, where he remained for three years. (In those days, one worked seven days a week, with no days off.

Joël Robuchon told me later that that was a bonus. It meant, at least, that you had a good square meal each day.)

As an apprentice, he did everything. He peeled vegetables, he prepared stocks, learned to open oysters to perfection, learned to identify the best beef and veal and to butcher the entire carcass, prepared his own foie gras, mopped floors and spent hour after hour polishing the heavy copper French pots that even today remain the centerpiece of his "batterie de cuisine."

Many of today's top chefs – Charles Barrier, Michel Guérard and Guy Savoy, to name just three – began their brilliant careers in the pastry kitchen.

And so did Joël Robuchon!

During those years of apprenticeship, he was assigned to one year of pastry work. It was a year that changed his life.

"After one year, I totally lost interest in pastry. Like so many fledgling chefs, the kitchen is where I wanted to be, not making tarts and cakes, ice creams and the like." Only recently did he realize, out loud, how much the experience influenced his technical form and the look of his cuisine.

Although today Joël Robuchon freely confesses his disinterest in pastry, few can compete with his creations.

● 1960 TO 1966:
THE AGE OF APPRENTICESHIP

In 1966, at the age of 21, Joël Robuchon became a Compagnon du Tour de France, beginning an invaluable traveling apprenticeship that allowed him to work with chefs all over France. It was also a time to test his physical prowess as a craftsman and his moral character as a human being, and learn, as he repeats time and again, "to value respect for work well done and for goals accomplished." (Only later, as a select member of the freemasons, would he go full circle with the challenge, complementing the manual nature of the compagnons with the intellectual and mental rigors of the franc-maçons.)

One restaurant after the other – Brittany's Grand Hôtel in Dinard, the Clos des Bernardins and Hôtel Berkeley in Paris –

"When you have been a pastry chef, you look at things differently. Your gestures and motions in the kitchen are not the same. You must be more exact, precise. Your work is all formula, all technique. And those qualities serve to help you, whether you're basting a chicken, deglazing a pan, or trussing a duck."

Years of intense labor and forced daily repetition – such as stuffing brochet and reconstituting freshwater pike, at The Berkeley in Paris – helped develop what Robuchon considers essential to any successful cook: the development of instinctive gestures that allow him to perfect cooking techniques. For once the chef is master of the technique he can do anything in the kitchen; he can learn to embroider, interpret and yes, even create those recipes he had learned by heart and made so many times they became part of his very fiber.

helped to form the foundation of his character.

Much like a fledgling artist who turns out copies of Manet and Monet, Van Gogh and Renoir, over and over and over again, until he begins to formulate, develop, and discover his own style, Robuchon kept on turning out sauce Béarnaise, omelets and scrambled eggs, grilled côtes de bœuf and pouleaupot Henri IV, and began to learn the supreme joy of working with the finest, freshest, most intelligently selected products that France, and the world, had to offer.

● 1967 TO 1974:
THE "BÊTE À CONCOURS"

When Joël Robuchon hit Paris in 1964, it was still, one needs to remember, the age of classicism, with giant brigades of chefs

stashed away in a basement kitchen, cooking over wood-burning stoves, required to accommodate elaborate menus laden with complicated dishes. He had the beginnings of a solid foundation, yet he was a long way from defining himself as a chef. This could well be considered his Marathon Man period, for these were the years in which he built himself up to be able to withstand the physical and mental challenges that would be presented to him and that he would present to himself.

To perfect his art, to turn himself into a cooking robot, as it were so that each gesture, each dish could be made almost with his eyes closed, Robuchon began entering (and winning) every competition imaginable, gathering bronze, silver and gold medals in competition after competition.

He didn't need the medals, he later noted, but needed the discipline and the training necessary to repeat a dish incessantly, all the while perfecting and all but memorizing it every gesture of the way.

Like the artist who no longer needs to copy Manet and Monet, Robuchon was just beginning to realize that he could create his own sauces, maybe make a lighter blini, improve upon a classic tart Tatin, even though in that era creation was not even considered one of the chef's options.

During this period, he met several of the men who remain influential today. At the Berkeley, Guy Ducret – who remains one of his right-hand men today – was part of his brigade. In 1969 he also began hearing talk of a man named Jean Delaveyne, then chef at the prominent La Camelia in the Paris suburb of Bougival, where he was known for his talent, passion and invention, as well as his strong, mercurial personality. "For me, Delaveyne was the first to help us move out from under the yoke of Escoffier – he was in truth the beginning of nouvelle cuisine, teaching me that cuisine was more than manual, more than technique, that it was also reflection," Robuchon muses.

"He was a culinary genius, the Van Gogh of the kitchen – capable of the very best and the very worst. But that in itself is a sign of genius. He influenced me by his intelligence, his research: the base of his cuisine was, yes, classic but it was well thought out." While these ideas may not sound revolutionary in 1996, twenty years

ago they were explosive. Robuchon goes on: "Delaveyne taught me that a chef is like an artist. If the artist doesn't know which colors to combine to achieve another color, he will never get what he's after. A chef is the same: if he does not have a solid classical base, if he does not know what an egg will do when you fry it, what a leg of lamb will do when you roast it, what will happen if you mix egg yolks with sugar, he will never be a good cook."

Along with Charles Barrier (recently retired from his legendary restaurant in Tours,) Delaveyne began to help Robuchon understand that beyond classical training, beyond

Benoît Guichard, a student of Paul Bocuse as well as a Meilleur Ouvrier de France, confides that he learns something new each day he works in Joël Robuchon's kitchen.

Early on, Robuchon always had a group of chefs around him that he depended upon and leaned on. He knew the success of even a small restaurant could never rest on the shoulders of a single man.

crawling out from under the influence of Escoffier, food had to do with taste, with essences and flavors.

This was a new world to the fledgling chef, as Delaveyne's creativity went wild, bringing spices and vinegar into a cuisine that had all but none, playing up the importance of acidity in a dish to add balance and aid enjoyment, as well as digestion.

"Delaveyne did things that seem insane to many, like adding tincture of iodine to boost the iodine-rich flavor of fish; he tossed out the classic veal stock that would sit around the kitchen all day and be used without thought as the base for each and every sauce. He taught us to think modern," insists Joël Robuchon.

From Barrier, his second spiritual father, he learned that, above all, the basis of all cuisine was the fresh produce. "Barrier was

the first to make his own foie gras to go out and find farmers who would produce it for him. He would to find the best – look into different flours for his own homemade bread." While Robuchon was being influenced by his mentors, he was slowly becoming a mentor himself to the rising chefs of today.

● 1977: JAPAN, A NEW INFLUENCE

In 1976, not long after Robuchon won the coveted Meilleur Ouvrier de France award (after failing in his first effort in 1974), fellow chef Paul Bocuse invited him to teach French cooking in Japan. "I was overwhelmed by the refinement of Japanese cuisine. And – despite what many assume – its total lack of sophistication," Robuchon recounts with amazement nearly twenty years later.

"The presentation of the food, the immense technical skills demanded in simply cutting the ingredients and then presenting them, impressed me. Soon I changed my presentations, they became simpler, and I began to appreciate the value of the presentation of a single, refined ingredient, all on its own."

At that stage in his career, a typical Robuchon dish might have included a roast partridge garnished with a tricolor assortment of rice, one white, one saffron, one pink, all lined up in strict, compact rows.

Today, Robuchon discards the flourish, pairing a roast guinea-hen with a flawless potato puree or a portion of perfect pasta, twisted gently into an even roll with a fork, working to honor the products themselves, with not a single extraneous element.

In return, the Japanese fell in love with his cuisine, admiring it for the same reasons he admired their style, with his emphasis on refinement, and rich, pure, unmasked flavors.

Before long, he was making regular teaching trips to Tokyo, where demonstration classes of 500 would sell out the day they were announced.

It was no surprise, then, that once his reputation was established in Japan, Robuchon felt confident teaming up with fellow Parisian restaurateur Jean-Claude Vrinat to create the elegant Restaurant Château Taillevent-Robuchon in Tokyo in 1994.

● 1981 TO 1993:
THE GLORIOUS YEARS AT JAMIN

Before 1981 – even in the culinary world – Joël Robuchon was far from being a household name. That all changed when, on December 15 1981 he opened his first restaurant on Paris' Rue de Longchamp. The restaurant had been named after a famous horse that raced at the Longchamp track, "Jamin," and Robuchon decided to maintain the name out of tradition. After one very shaky month, when he sometimes served less than ten diners a day, the press and word of mouth soon made sure the tables were filled night and day. From January 15 1982, Robuchon played to a packed house, lunch and dinner, five days each week.

The 110- and 210-franc menus, written in a lean, Asiatic script and featuring a mysteriously dreamy rendering of a top-hatted "compagnon," were veritable bargains, with low-budget products such as "laitances de hareng" (soft herring roe) and "joues de raie"

There has been a long history of mutual admiration and influence-between Joël Robuchon and Japan, where he has opened a restaurant.

Joël Robuchon first came to Japan to find inspiration. Today his influence finds its way to the Tokyo kitchens of his own restaurant.

The attentiveness of Joël Robuchon and his team in the kitchen, and the care of Jean-Claude Vrinat in the dining room make Château Taillevent-Robuchon one of the finest restaurants in the world.

(skate cheeks) also appearing on the menu. They certainly helped keep the reservation list alive, though Robuchon's ballooning reputation could probably have kept the restaurant afloat with high-priced menu selections exclusively. A review of the menus from those twelve years reveals much about the evolution of this brilliant chef.

You see ingredients popping on and off the menu. You witness a move from the less noble to the more noble. And you note the creation of "theme" menus celebrating a single luxury ingredient, be it black truffles, fresh morels, or the entire panoply of shellfish, or crustaceans. And you begin to see the birth, growth and evolution of many of the dishes that have made him famous today, including the silky potato puree (on the menu from the very first day,) the "Gelée de caviar à la crème de chou-fleur" (making its debut in August 1984) and the "Galette de truffes aux oignons et lard fumé" (first cited in his first all-truffle menu in December 1985,) later to be transformed into the "Tarte friande aux truffes."

Joël Robuchon's style is unique: no other chef in the world turns out dishes with such military precision, distinguished by glossy veneers and such intense, concentrated flavors. The tidiness of the plate reflects the tidiness of the spirit of the creator. His style consists of combining many little things that, on their own, may not stand for much. But it is the calculated addition of many small items that adds up to one large and full-flavored dish.

While beef in various guises – sauced simply with an emulsion of red wine and black pepper, shallots, herbs, or a mix of herbs and shallots – appears on his very first menu and remains there for the first year, it never returns. Like many chefs, Robuchon simply finds French beef uninteresting, of uneven quality and thus not dependable. For many of the same reasons, veal had long been ignored by the temples of French gastronomy. But in 1985, Robuchon was introduced to Robert Fabre, the dedicated veal farmer and butcher from Aurillac in the Auvergne, and soon his signature côte de veau, a luscious, double-thick veal chop, appeared on the menu, accompanied by a simple and classic pairing of wild morel mushrooms and thin green asparagus.

Throughout the Jamin period, Bresse poultry, sweetbreads, lamb and duck filled out the meat portion of the menu, while fish, shellfish and pasta always took center stage.

In 1981, few restaurants made their own bread, but Joël Robuchon's reverence for what he considers "la nourriture par excellence" convinced him to send pastry chef Philippe Gobet off to bread-baking school, and soon each Jamin diner was consuming at least two crusty, yeasty rolls per meal. From the early days of Jamin, Robuchon's lack of interest in sweets and his total confidence in pastry chef Philippe Gobet allowed him to delegate that portion of the menu. Yet you could see Robuchon's influence in each dessert, even on the rolling pastry cart, which was filled with such delicacies as a rich chocolate tart, glorious lime-flavored crêpes soufflées, a perfect apple and raisin tart, and supremely rich ice-creams.

Everything was technically perfect, visually appealing, and impeccably fresh.

Soon Robuchon was making trips to Limoges to visit master porcelain manufacturer Michel Bernardaud, coaxing him to create special soup bowls for what would become Robuchon's growing variety of revolutionary and astonishing entrées, beginning with his "Crème de coques et de palourdes en soupière" (a delicate cream that combines tender baby clams with prized medium-size clams) and ending with his signature "Gelée de caviar à la crème de choufleur" (Lobster aspic and caviar with cauliflower cream). All the while, Robuchon's cooking became more and more defined,

more expressive, more creative. One could see the growing refinement not just on the plate (as dishes became simpler, more streamlined, but no less haunting or delicious), but in the titles of the dishes themselves, which turned lucidly poetic, as with the fresh cod fried with herbs and "Marinière de fins coquillages (Shellfish marinière) à la fleur de thyme." He revolutionized the modern definition of soups with his series of creamy, multi-textued openers, such as his "Crème d'huîtres aux pointes d'asperges vertes" (Cream of oyster and green asparagus soup) and his "Soupe chaude à la gelée de poule" (Warm soup of foie gras and chicken jelly.)

His food began to take on very round

And always, there was this military-like precision of each plate: the tiny dots, the tiny squares, the architectural elements that added flavor, texture and harmony.

No less than three competent sommeliers were employed at any one time at Joël Robuchon's, where the selection wines and liqueurs were as important as the cuisine.

forms, symbols perhaps of the unity and completeness he was feeling at the time. Soon galettes and tarts became part of his vocabulary, not just in the sweet fare, but the savory as well. We saw the birth of his "Tarte renversée de pommes de terre au foie gras" (Upside-down foie gras and potato tart) and the early inspiration of his now-famous truffle tart with the "Galette de truffe au lard fumé."

Tiny dots of chlorophyll and infinitesimal cubes of vegetables were not simple garnishes, but those almost invisible elements worked to produce the intense tastes that have made his reputation. There were, in fact, no garnishes as we traditionally knew

them, for those three perfect leaves of chervil were not there as points of beauty, but as an ingredient that, once on our palate, would help unify the remaining ingredients in the dish.

The harmony of flavors was carried on through to the wine list, which featured a wealth of Burgundies and Bordeaux, and also a carefully selected group of wines from the Rhone, the wine region that Robuchon considers best reflects his food.

"My cuisine can't withstand a wine that is too strong or dominant," he says during a conversation with his longtime sommelier, Antoine Hernandez. They both prefer elegant whites – such as white Châteauneuf-du-Pape and Condrieu with shellfish; and character-filled reds such as Côte-Rôtie, Hermitage or Châteauneuf-du-Pape for game, poultry and meat. "Wine should never be superior to a dish," but rather should always play a harmonious role with the rest of the menu.

Within just three months of opening Jamin, the restaurant was awarded its first Michelin star, after over a year, its second, and in just two years, the third, coveted Michelin star was awarded, the fastest rise in Michelin history.

With characteristic modesty – enforced by years as a compagnon – Robuchon likes to say that the award did not mean he had earned the third star, it only meant he had earned the right to work toward justifying it.

During the Jamin years, the commercial food industry (Fleury Michon) came calling, hoping that it could convince Robuchon to wave his magic wand over a new line of packaged dinners. "Each time I said no. The commercial food industry simply did not interest me. Then one day, I did meet with them, and the ideas sounded feasible. But when I found out that Fleury Michon's small factory was only 15 kilo-meters from Mauléon, the village of my childhood seminary, I knew that fate must have decided I would work for them."

Joël Robuchon is like a good guide. In the kitchen, he looks out for his brigade the way a father looks after his brood. Often, his decisions were not obvious at the time, such as sending his important right-hand man, Maurice Guillouët, off to Australia in 1985. In retrospect, it's clear that Robuchon knew back then that one day he would need a chef of his own in Japan, one on whom he could depend fully, and one who already had under his toque a wealth of foreign experience, preferably in Asia.

Joël Robuchon listens and he responds. People flock to Robuchon for advice, for consolation, for a needed pep talk, much the way the faithful flock to a church for the comfort of the priest's words in the

From the early days, Robuchon was impressed by the necessity and power of a dependable, talented brigade. He surrounded himself with people he could count on every step of the way.

confessional. But the mentor also needs his support group: one group that has provided immense support is the select organization of *francs-maçons*, or Masons, men from all walks of life, many of whom have became close friends.

The group has not only helped him to strive to give the maximum of himself each day, but it expanded his contact with the world outside of cooking.

The secrecy of the group has caused many to look for visual signs or symbols on his plates, searching for an outward reflection of the *franc-maçon* life in the decoration of a dish, but Robuchon insists that it simply is not there.

"The only *franc-maçon* reflection in my work is that I constantly strive; my work is permanent research, permanent obsession with the quality of one's labor," he explains.

Despite his fame and high standing – by the mid-80's he was already being called the greatest chef in the world – Robuchon continued to be influenced by those around him, especially fellow three-star chefs, Alain

Chapel and Fredy Girardet. From these two, particularly Chapel, he began to understand what he likes to call "la vraie cuisine du goût," the cuisine of true flavors. In speaking of Chapel, he says: "When we were together, we never stopped talking. We'd talk and talk about flavors, about technique, how to coax refinement and delicacy out of any ingredient and into our food," he relates, almost wistfully.

Joël Robuchon often brings up the death of Alain Chapel – of a heart attack at the age of 50 – as a warning signal for himself.

His other major source of inspiration was Fredy Girardet of Crissier, Switzerland.

"I know that it seems like an obvious goal for a modern chef, but Girardet really taught me to go with the flow of the season, to be tough with my suppliers," he explains.

To this day, there is one ingredient – fresh cream – that stumps him. He detests the texture and flavor of today's version and misses the sweet, mildly acidic perfume of the fresh creams of yesterday. Robuchon uses little cream in his cooking, because the only good cream he finds today is sent to him from time to time by none other than Fredy Girardet.

The clearest way to understand the evolution of his work during the Jamin years is to follow the evolution of a single signature dish, his "Gelée de caviar à la crème de choufleur," Creamy cauliflower soup topped with a perfect, quenelle-shaped spoonful of caviar.

With this evolution you see that, like in his life, Robuchon does nothing haphazardly, nothing out of a quick inspiration. Each dish that arrives at a diner's table has been worked through many times, fiddled with, modified,

The Jamin dining room grew to a staff of twenty, and the kitchen brigade grew to more than twenty-five chefs. Among them were several of today's top students, including Maurice Guillouët and Benoît Guichard who still exhibit the now famous Robuchon characteristics in their kitchen: a fanatic commitment to technical perfection, extraordinary reflexes, and that rare ability to season a dish with carefully practiced gestures.

"A truly good cook should be able to produce the same quality, whether it be for ten or for ten thousand. My catering training at the large hotels, where we did dinners for thousands in far from ideal kitchens, also relates directly to my work with Fleury Michon. I am proud to participate in restoring value and importance to everyday French home cooking, so that the French can eat better and better.

Working for Fleury Michon, I am not just a name on a poster, but a true creator, innovator, researcher!"

modified some more, and finally transformed into the dish that Robuchon had in his head.

The dish began simply, as a desire to mimic the Russian tradition of combining sour cream with caviar.

The daily scene: before delivering each dish to the dining room, waiters stand by patiently for Joël Robuchon's examination and approval of its preparation and presentation.

Robuchon loved the idea of the unctuousness, the bold acidity of the cream contrasting with the salty, bitter, faintly sweet flavor of the caviar. He fiddled, he modified. He first thought of a velouté, a thick traditional cream base for the soup, and began with a fish stock base. Not bitter enough. Looking for a more intense bitterness, he turned to white asparagus, with its dominantly bitter edge. The dish first appeared on the menu in August 1984. Thirteen years later it remains a Robuchon signature.

All this glory and talk of perfection lead one to wonder: are there any chinks in his armor, any weak spots to the genius?

"I am not capable of spontaneity," he says, explaining that for him, each dish must be carefully considered, each ingredient measured, each gesture studied, planned and controlled.

In Joël Robuchon's kitchen, faces bear many emotions: from exhaustion to curiosity, camaraderie, to intense concentration. When you realize these chefs give their best day after day, ten performances each week, forty-eight weeks a year, it's not surprising that one finds few old chefs in the kitchen today.

●1994 TO 1996: EXPRESSION & CREATION, AVENUE POINCARÉ

For years Robuchon was frustrated by the modest size of his kitchen as well as the modest decor of the dining room at Jamin. So continually he searched for another Parisian address that would fulfill his dreams of a vast, expansive kitchen, with a dining room that reflected the refinement and excellence of his own cuisine.

He found it in an opulent Art Nouveau townhouse on the bourgeois Avenue Raymond-Poincaré in the 16th arrondissement. With regrets, Jamin's last dinner was served in December 1993 and doors opened just a few weeks later at Restaurant Joël Robuchon on Avenue Raymond-Poincaré.

When Robuchon moved from Jamin to restaurant Joël Robuchon, he hoped to clean house, make a fresh start. He had been serving potato puree for years, and wanted to move on. But diners would not allow it.

During the last few weeks of Jamin, customers became downright nostalgic. They began begging: "You certainly won't take the potatoes, or the lamb, or the mer-lan en colère off the menu?"

"I realized that I couldn't start a fresh.

There was too much identity, too much emotion attached to many of the dishes," Robuchon explained early in 1994.

The next two years spent at the new restaurant – which offered grander space and more illustrious surroundings – also allowed Joël Robuchon a few moments of creative freedom. "What I'm going to serve you tonight will be bizarre, maybe downright wacky. Maybe you won't even like it," he would often say to me and my friend, in the tiny alcove near the restaurant's kitchen,

Joël Robuchon has always considered that the presentation of a dish was just as important as the elements on the plate.

"One eats through one's eyes," he likes to say, noting that one's first impression is formed when a dish is set in front of them. One looks, and then one smells.

Tasting is only the third and final step of one's evaluation of a dish.

He is like a master perfumer, who knows what each and every scent and flower will do, and what they will do in combination. His final creations employ all his artistic skills in order to capture flavors, fix essential tastes, distill the pleasures for the senses.

which was a quiet spot Joël Robuchon reserved for lunches with his wife, or those he wanted to use as "guinea pigs" for his newest dishes. It was clear that the master had reached one goal in his life and, though he continued to fiddle, tinker and modify, he also clearly felt the freedom to create and even shock from time to time.

Soon diners were introduced to his "plats du voyage," dishes inspired by trips to Asia or to Provence, such as coriander-rich chicken soup that surpassed anything a Chinese master might dream up.

But mostly, they were treated to traditional Robuchon: studied, refined, considered and put out onto the platter for all to see. He worked towards and achieved what has been called a "cuisine invisible," a cuisine made up of many parts and sometimes seemingly contradictory flavors that are almost miraculously merged into a cohesive, flavorful whole.

Robuchon's food has set itself apart by its complexity. "If it was simple, anyone could do it," is his standard response. Yet he never pursues complexity for complexity's sake.

Certain goals have been achieved, but at 51 years of age, the master is still part *compagnon*, walking purposefully down that road to perfection.

● A GLANCE AT THE MASTER'S ATELIER

Over the years, I have spent hours and hours observing Robuchon and his staff in

In Joël Robuchon's kitchens, there is always an almost monastic silence.

The fact that Joël Robuchon was not present in the kitchen every second of the day does not mean that details got by him. Once it came time for the food to make its passage from the kitchen to the table, he was always there, at "the pass," eyeing every single item – even the toast and butter that accompanied a dish!

his kitchens. In the early days of Jamin (the early 1980's), the kitchen was a riot of activity, with chefs bunched elbow-to-elbow into an incredibly small space. I remember that the pastry chef, Philippe Gobet, came to work at 5 am, so he could have full use of the ovens before the rest of the cooks arrived. Robuchon was tough on his staff, very tough.

I recall one morning when the youngest and newest of the staff was preparing the day's meal for the staff: he was roasting several large roasts of pork. As he opened the oven door to baste the meat, Robuchon happened to walk past and screamed at the young chef: "Is that the way you were taught to baste meat? I can't believe it. Any house-wife on the street could do better than you!" The ultimate insult, I am sure, for a young chef who must have been elated to have reached the lowest rank of the highest kitchen in the world. I once asked one of the chefs if it bothered him, being scolded and corrected dozens of times each day. "Not at all," he replied, "for I learn something new here every single day."

● **ADVICE FOR THE HOME COOK**

Curiously, if one examines the scrupulousness and attention to detail Robuchon demands in his own restaurant kitchen, one

can also find that they provide many helpful guidelines for the home cook.

For in the end, most of what comes out of any kitchen – professional or amateur – is measured less in complex technique and more in careful organization and selection of quality ingredients.

For instance, when preparing a simple green salad, he mixes many kinds of greens and herbs and cuts each into bite-size pieces.

This way, with each bite, we taste many flavors, not just one. One learns quickly that the whole is greater than the sum of its parts. Likewise, complex does not always translate to mean difficult. For example, in one of his older, classic recipes for zucchini-

wrapped shrimp, a greater depth of flavors is achieved by the use of differents fats.

A light peanut oil is used to cooked highly flavored chanterelle mushrooms, sweet butter for delicate oyster mushrooms, and rich goose fat to enhance the shrimp. In the end, when the ingredients are combined on the fork for a single bite, you end up with flavors that seem to say, two plus two equals one hundred! (if the same dish was prepared with, say, only peanut oil, or only goose fat, the result would simply not be the same.)

So it is not madness after all. Nor is it all foie gras and truffles. But rather a studied and intelligent approach to food. It is an approach that teaches you that whispers of

Joël Robuchon and the maître d'hôtel consulted each day before the day's service. Success, as they both know, is in the details.

In watching Joël Robuchon cook, one learned that fat "fixes" flavor, forming a sort of protective shield so that essences are not lost in cooking. Best of all, cooks learned that you do not need a lot of fat to stabilize the flavor of a single ingredient.

chervil and thyme are not merely decorative garnishes, but develop the flavor of a dish.

It's knowing that parsley snipped with a pair of scissors will have a more intense flavor than the same herb chopped with a knife.

It's realizing that food that's seasoned after cooking and just before serving will require less seasoning, and will offer more heightened, direct flavors. Rather than tasting salty, the food will taste well seasoned. It is also realizing that those extra moments spent straining a sauce, waiting for dough to chill, scraping the seeds from a vanilla bean, peeling a pepper, or garnishing a tart, are not a waste of time at all. They are sophisticated culinary investments that pay you back with the very first bite.

● ON FIXING FLAVORS

"Fixing the flavors of food is something you cannot teach," Robuchon has told me time and again. "And it is one of the hardest concepts to teach a young chef. How do you go about teaching when an ingredient is at its peak?"

"When cooking truffles or mushrooms, for example, it may be as simple as knowing exactly when to cover the pot, so that the essences and flavors do not evaporate into thin air," he explains. Robuchon likes to use the analogy of preparing a cup of tea.

There is a moment at which one brews exactly the perfect amount of tea in the perfect amount of water at the perfect temperature for the perfect amount of time.

That is perfectly brewed tea.

Brew it a few seconds less and it is underbrewed – you have not captured the essence of the tea leaves. Allow it to brew a few seconds more, and the tea will be overbrewed – you will have a bitter, overly steeped brew.

When the tea is perfectly brewed, you are treating it with the greatest respect and knowledge, and the result is a drink that allows the tea to impart a maximum of flavor and the greatest enjoyment.

● ON SEASONING

If a cook learns only one concept from studying Robuchon's cooking, it should be seasoning.

The major criticism I have of most chefs is their inability to season well. Robuchon's rules are simple.

Season lightly, all along the way. But season from beginning to end.

In preparing a simple roast chicken, for example, he advises seasoning the bird inside and out just before it is put into the oven. (If seasoned too far in advance, the salt will draw essential juices from the poultry, and tend to denature it.)

Once the chicken is cooked, it is seasoned again, before it is set to rest.

This final seasoning will allow the salt and pepper to be lightly absorbed by the skin, giving the chicken a very freshly seasoned, "finished" flavor.

● THE WORLD ACCORDING TO ROBUCHON

Once, during a cooking class, a student asked Joël Robuchon if it really made such a difference if, say, one didn't take the time to season that chicken at the end, or let it stand tail in the air for 15 minutes so that the juices would run down into the breast meat, making it moist and

more tender. His response was totally logical and yet unexpected: "None of the details is critical in and of itself. But it is the accumulation of these details that make the difference between a mediocre dish and a successful one." Many people talk about perfection and perfectionism. In my entire life I have met only one perfectionist: Joël Robuchon.

And even he does not boast of being a perfectionist, but claims to be a man in eternal search of that elusive goal. I have seen him prepare flawless banquets for total strangers. Is it the pursuit for satisfaction over a job well done that drives him? I doubt it. But within, there is the obsession, the habitude, the religion, if you will, of doing the best you can with every task, no matter how little or how large.

In the large and luxurious setting of his restaurant on avenue Raymond-Poincaré, Robuchon reached the summit of his life, taking full advantage of a generous amount of space and freedom.

The entry allowed the first visual exchange with the client. At Joël Robuchon's, it was granted a good deal of importance. Every element of the table was in place. Just as in the kitchen, everything was carefully planned, nothing is left to chance, every detail examined under the careful eye of the maître d'hôtel.

● DIARY OF A DAY IN THE KITCHEN WITH JOËL ROBUCHON

Seldom is one aware that while there is great drama and theater in the dining room, there is drama of another sort going on behind those swinging kitchen doors. What follows is a patchwork diary of a morning's visit.

8 AM. The ovens at the restaurant have been fired up since 5 am, when the first pastry chef arrived. The chefs, I know, will be here until midnight, with maybe an hour's break in the late afternoon.

9:15 AM. A brigade of sixteen spotless cooks with chef's whites and toques bob up and down in a lovely, free-form ballet. The kitchen is already in full swing: veal stock simmers on a back burner, while the gentle rhythm of steel knives striking wooden chopping blocks resounds through the air.

10:35 AM. All is surprisingly calm. The fish delivery man has just arrived, and it's as if a salty sea breeze rolled in. Mingling with the aroma of a simmering tomato sauce, it's pure heaven.

I watch Robuchon, and think of him in a roomful of toys.

You can almost see the complex wheels in his brain whirling about as he contemplates the creation of a new dish.

Eric, a trim, tiny, impeccably organized chef is lost in his own world, meticulously rolling out sheets of pasta so thin you can see through them.

Alongside, Moushi, a Japanese chef, prepares the fresh langoustines and truffles that will form the interior of a dreamy ravioli.

"Set aside a bit of pasta for me, I want to try something this morning," Robuchon tells Eric, proceding to cut little rounds the diameter of a 25-cent coin.

1:34 PM The crazy hour! Even a mere observer of the activities of the morning would absorb the overwhelming tension that reigned in the kitchen.

The chef's most important instruments lie in the senses that make him human: touch, hearing, smell, sight and taste.

He twists each end, so it resembles a little bow.

Then he lets the pasta rest to dry, and turns to more pressing details.

He plans to serve the fresh little bows of pasta with great slivers of fresh black truffles.

10:45 AM. Joël Robuchon roams the room. He tastes, he samples, he inquires. I never saw a chef who tasted as much as he does. With his staff, he is part lamb and part lion. None of this proper French distance for him. But there is no question as to who is the boss.

11:15 AM. Copper saucepans, bubbling with hot liquids, are shuttled quickly from one bank of stoves to another. Together,

Robuchon and his staff review the day's reservation list.

Today the 15 tables await Spaniards, Italians, Americans, and of course, French. As orders come in, the nationality of each diner is noted.

That's because well-cooked means one thing to the Spanish, another to the French, and yet another to the American diner.

Robuchon winces as Benoît takes the ravioli from the water – the bows have retained their form and they're perfectly cooked. What a relief! Even three-star chefs have to work at their creations.

NOON. Two hundred and fifty shiny brown dinner rolls are about to come out of

Joël Robuchon renews the menu every three months: "It prevents the kitchen from becoming too self-satisfied. As soon as a dish becomes set in a routine, we have to change it. Having the restaurant booked up at lunchtime and in the evening makes that easier. The chefs are able to anticipate the next sitting: they know how many fish to expect, how many lobsters to prepare, which meats to get ready. There are fewer surprises and we can thus ensure that only absolutely fresh produce is served. In any case, one always has to find a way to motivate the chefs, to stimulate them with change and renewal; it is the best way of bringing out their talent to the fullest."

Lunch on the run: a young dishwasher races through the kitchen as well as his lunch, not missing a beat during the most hectic part of the workday.

the oven. They are gorgeous. For many chefs, bread is just a slice of something to sop up sauces. Not for Robuchon.

The dessert trolley is arranged. The pastry chef is still putting the finishing touches on a fresh raspberry tart.

The raspberries were picked this morning, attention to freshness is essential. But still, amazing!

1:33 PM. The steam of simmering pots is replaced by a thin, gentle veil of smoke. Tension is high, faces are flushed. I feel as though I am watching a Charlie Chaplin film, speeded up for special effect.

Bodies dart from one end of the kitchen to the other. How is it no one runs into anyone else?

I made a note of all the dishes Benoît is trying to juggle. There is a "Civet de lapin" (Jugged rabbit) in the oven, he has just been passed an order for three pigeons (two rare, one medium,) and he must keep tasting and adjusting the seasoning on the half a dozen sauces he hovers over at the stove.

Robuchon calls for seconds of the "Tête de cochon" (Pig's head), and, in the midst of it all, a diner sends back an order of veal kidneys. The guest decided that, after all, he wasn't so fond of organ meat.

It's enough to make everyone stomp out of the kitchen. Nobody does.

1:37 PM. Robuchon is angry. "Who did this to me? Who did this to me? Who cut the lamb like this? Not you Eric, surely!"

"You'll never touch my lamb again. This is the work of an apprentice!"

Robuchon slams his hand on the counter and stalks away, visibly upset. The kitchen is momentarily silent. Heads are hung low. The lamb is returned to Eric. The diner will have to wait a few more seconds to sample this attempt at perfection.

2:05 PM. "Table twelve loved the Mashed Potatoes. They want seconds."

Robuchon beams. If the customer asks for seconds, that must mean he loves the dish.

"Un supplément de purée de pommes de terre! (Mashed Potatoes) Chaude! Chaude! Bien chaude!" he shouts with a touch of glee in his voice.

2:20 PM. Dishes are everywhere. Occupying every available spot in the kitchen.

They're stacked on shelves in the oven, set in neat rows along the edges of the stove as each chef adds his garnish, his final touch. I make a mental note of my favorite dish here: the fresh codfish studded with smoked salmon! Who else could take a poor man's fish and raise it to such heights?

3:18 PM. The kitchen, at last, is calming down. There is still much to do. Every centimeter must be scrubbed and polished to a mirror shine. Robuchon and the chefs discuss the menus for the following day.

I glance at the clock and realize they have all been pushing themselves to the limit since early this morning. And they will do it again tonight, tomorrow and the next day. In the end, one knows, it is a small price to pay for a shot at perfection.

From his masters, Joël Robuchon learned what it meant to be exigent, overwhelmingly disciplined, to keep a kitchen fanatically hygienic, and how to master the economics of a kitchen. "In the kitchen, you have to learn a lot to know a little."

3:48 PM: Lunch is over, and the kitchen falls into a silence resembling a church after services.

July 5 1996: the final page in the Robuchon diary – the final press clips and the very last clients. Below right, mail and telegrams came from around the world to celebrate the chef's final day.

It is the last toast in the kitchen, where an enormous amount of talent, knowledge and know-how is gathered. Faces show a huge palette of contradictory emotions: euphoria, sadness, nostalgia…

Philippe Groult ceremonially delivers the last dish served on July 5 1996, repeating his gesture from 1981, when he delivered the first dish to the dining room at the now legendary Jamin.

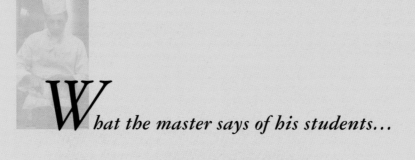

What the master says of his students...

"**Dominique Bouchet** gave up his lustrous career in Paris to return to his native Charente, where he executes a fresh and simple style of cuisine totally devoid of pretense."

"**Christophe Cussac** is the "accidental chef," the son of a restaurateur who worked as my secretary before following in the family tradition. He is a man of many facets, who became a cook out of sheer desire and passion."

"**Philippe Groult** is a young man who began with nothing and built his brilliant career slowly and progressively. Independent and ambitious, he is a man of principle and integrity."

"**Benoît Guichard** has been an essential member of my team from the earliest days of Jamin. He is a man of honor and morality and one of my most prized associates. His modesty, commitment to excellence, and his ability to clearly execute my cuisine and my ideas make him an exemplary chef. In the kitchen, when Benoît speaks, everyone listens."

"**Maurice Guillouët** is the ideal foreign associate. His experience with me in Paris, and his perfect understanding of Asian cuisine and ingredients make him a true ambassador for French cuisine in Japan."

Of all Joël Robuchon's pupils, Dominique Bouchet is undoubtedly the one with the most independent cooking style. At 43 years of age, the chef-owner of the Michelin two-star "Moulin de Marcouze," in his native Charente, has been away from Robuchon's kitchen for nearly twenty years, and is ready to reflect on his experiences.

"Robuchon taught me a lot about cooking – that is, about the strength and rigor that one needs to be a great cook – but even more impressive was his way with people, his psychology. "

Bouchet joined the Robuchon brigade at the opening of the Hôtel Concorde-Lafayette in 1974. Within four years, Bouchet worked his way up to chef. In 1978, Robuchon called him to take over the kitchens of Jamin.

Dominique Bouchet ● *Le Moulin de Marcouze*

In 1981, Bouchet's life was turned upside down once again: "Mr. Robuchon told me that I should take the position as chef at The Tour d'Argent." By 1988, after eight years as chef, Bouchet was ready for a place of his own. "I learned a lot about maintaining standards at the Tour, but I wanted my freedom to cook what I wanted."

His cooking is the simplest of all Robuchon's students, and reflects a total absence of pretense or false sophistication. "Robuchon knew how to get the best from every person on his staff," explains Bouchet. "He was more like the coach of an athletic team."

In addition to the success of his restaurant in France, Bouchet also has close ties with Japan, having made more than 130 trips to Tokyo as a French culinary ambassador, teaching and consulting with various Japanese groups."I love the Japanese emphasis on refinement, their obsession with freshness, the cleanliness and high standards of work, but I don't like their food," he says with utter frankness. Bouchet's success does not leave Joël Robuchon without regrets: "With him, there was always something to learn, a new complexity revealed. It was difficult to leave that behind. "

CHRISTOPHE CUSSAC ● *L'Abbaye Saint-Michel*

under the direction of chef Philippe Groult. "During the first six months, Christophe Cussac cried after every service," relates Robuchon with tenderness, "but that's what made him strong and helped him to find his own voice and style. He became a real G.I."

In 1983, at almost 30 years of age, with a comprehensive understanding of Robuchon's style, Cussac would leave the kitchens of Jamin for another three star Michelin kitchen, Troisgros in Roanne. "I needed another experience, I did not want my style of cooking to come from only one kitchen."

His year at Troisgros not only took him outside of the realm of Parisian cooking, but also familiarized him with the products of Burgundy. In 1984, he assumed responsibility for his parents' restaurant, "L'Abbaye Saint-Michel" in Tonnerre, where today he holds the two, coveted Michelin stars.

However, even within the confines of his own kitchen, Cussac retains the influence of his master.

"When I make a dish for my menu," explains Cussac, "I taste it and ask myself what criticism Robuchon might offer were he to taste it himself." In this sense, Cussac has succeeded in using the foundation of his knowledge, gleaned from the teachings of Robuchon, but has blended it with his own personal touch. "He would tell us how he envisioned the dish and what the taste and the marriage of flavors was to be," elaborates Cussac. "The rest was up to us to figure out. And that's what made me who I am."

Having begun his career as Joël Robuchon's secretary in the kitchens of the Hôtel Concorde-Lafayette during the 1970's, Christophe Cussac shares perhaps the most intimate relationship with the master from among all his pupils. Since his association began not as a youthful manual aide, but as one who oversaw every element of a major operation – from ordering supplies to bookkeeping details – Cussac was offered a rare glimpse into another world of the master.

But soon, at Robuchon's encouragement, Cussac added kitchen experience to his dossier and began his career at Jamin in 1981,

PHILIPPE GROULT ● *L'Amphyclès*

To make a dream come true, first you have to have a dream. Philippe Groult's dream was to follow in Robuchon's footsteps and someday join the elite club of Michelin three-star chefs. "I had to succeed, I simply had to."

The seeds of the dream were planted and grew during his eight years at Robuchon's side, first at the Concorde-Lafayette, then at the Hotel Nikko. In 1981, at the age of 26, Groult was appointed chef at the newly opened Jamin, beginning a high-pressure period during which Groult describes, "Robuchon was the head, and I became his two legs."

He recalls a day when he was ordered to cook a filet of beef. He was chef of the kitchen, but Robuchon sent it back to him four times before the master was satisfied.

Groult had been humiliated in front of his brigade, but realized in time that this had been no idle temper tantrum, but a challenge to perfection.

Today Groult is the master of the ambitious Amphycles in Paris. He's hoping to develop even further his own personal style, although his cuisine remains clearly reflective of his master's influence in terms of simplicity of style, as well as intensity of flavors. But beyond ingredients, technique, and presentation, the most valuable lesson Groult learned from Robuchon was that of administration and management. With Groult one sees that the master never stops teaching, or demanding the best of his pupils. "When Robuchon helped me secure the initial loan for my restaurant, I realized that I had a responsibility to him as well as to myself." Groult laid the groundwork for excellence by winning numerous culinary awards and in 1982, he became a Meilleur Ouvrier de France. Even now, after seven years on his own, Groult, 43 years old, still regularly seeks the advice of his master. "If I have a question, a doubt, I know I can go to him. And that's a nice feeling after all this time."

Benoît Guichard ● *Restaurant Jamin*

ever-present trance-like gaze – as though he is so immersed in his thoughts and gestures, he is unaware of all else around him. But he is in perfect control of himself and each person in the brigade.

Like his master, he would not ask another to fulfill a task he himself could not carry out to perfection.

Of all Robuchon's students he is the closest to understanding the master's obsession with perfection. Watch his gestures as he painstakingly salts each and every morsel of tomato confit, reflectively turns the scallops on a grill. His favorite quote comes from 18th century pastry chef Marie-Antoine Carême: "In the kitchen, there are not many principles, only one. And that is to satisfy the client."

Because Guichard has not had a day on his own since returning to the Robuchon kitchens in 1987, he is the most "marked" by the master and the least free to create a cuisine of his own. Yet like Robuchon in his early years, those restrictions have also allowed him the freedom to technically perfect his craft.

Of all Joël Robuchon's students, Benoît Guichard has reigned longest in the role of "chef." He has steered the ship from the days of Jamin, piloting it through the move days to Raymond-Poincaré, remaining steadily dependable to the closing days of Restaurant Joël Robuchon.

His discipline, intense concentration, and deep moral code are pure Robuchon. Glance at Guichard in the kitchen, and you'll see that permanent, almost rigid, bent-over posture. He appears to have an intimate relationship with each ingredient he handles, protecting it, not quite willing to let it go. There is that

Thus Guichard's sole, essential role for nearly a decade has been that of the "good soldier." And that he has been, helping Robuchon perfect the art of vacuum cooking, and earning the coveted "Meilleur Ouvrier de France" award.

Like Robuchon, Guichard was often propelled and guided by sheer gourmandize: what started as a passion for good food turned into a profession.

In 1981, when Brittany-born Maurice Guillouët made his Paris debut at the "Tour d'Argent," the chef at the helm was none other than Robuchon-trained Dominique Bouchet. Guillouët didn't stay long on the Left Bank, however. For soon after hearing talk of the talents of the new chef of Jamin, Guillouët knocked on Robuchon's door and found a welcome home. Within a year he was chef de partie of the fish section. Only two years later, at the age of 23, this tall, lean, quiet and introspective chef was named Jamin's chef de cuisine, a day he refers to as "the most memorable moment of my career."

Robuchon all but nudged Guillouët out the door, arranging for him a new world, a new experience, a new life. Thus Guillouët left the kitchen of Jamin in 1990, headed for a job as chef at the Hotel Nikko in Sydney, Australia, where the wealth of fish and shellfish and a more casual lifestyle allowed him to spread his wings and begin to express his own style of cooking. Sydney also provided a cultural experience that would prepare Guillouët for cooking outside of France, another building block of culinary knowledge.

Just as the foods of diverse cultures find their way into the fundamentally French cuisine of Joël Robuchon, so must his chefs understand these other cultures. In 1992, Guillouët become chef de cuisine at Restau-

M AURICE GUILLOUËT ● *Château Taillevent-Robuchon*

rant Taillevent-Robuchon in Tokyo, undisputedly the most highly reputed French restaurant in Japan.

Although Taillevent-Robuchon is situated in Tokyo, the menu is faithful to the foundations of French cooking and the celebration of its products. "There is not a single gesture in my work that does not make me think of Robuchon," relates Guillouët. "The most important ability I learned from him was how to taste, taste, taste, and how to coax a dish into tasting delicious. I carry that with me wherever I go."

Products

AND PRODUCERS

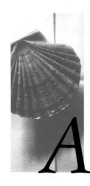

A journey to the land of exceptional flavors

Think of a painter and his palette: the artist prepares his canvas, carefully takes out his paint brushes, looks out at the landscape, and his mission has begun. But as he gazes at the different hues and textures on the horizon, he turns to his palette and entreats the colors to speak for him.

The same challenge – that same blank canvas – lies before every cook as he creates a dish. Each dish, each marriage, each subtlety, relies upon the products. The artist Joël Robuchon has selected the colors that have been used to create the palette of this book, the products that celebrate the dif-

ferent regions of France, its varied seasons and, most importantly, Robuchon's own evolution as a chef. The creation of a cuisine begins with the earth and the local products it has to offer – their quality, their freshness. Similarly, an understanding of ingredients in their natural state is the first step to creating a cuisine that transcends the ordinary.

In the opinion of chef Robuchon, the choice of products should and must be the primary interest, the greatest concern of any cook, whether it is a woman preparing a simple meal for her family, or a grand chef working with the most noble ingredients.

And that is the goal of this book – a book based on the selection of eight products by Joël Robuchon and the five pupils he chose to give their interpretation of each. Some of the ingredients form the very foundation of French cooking – truffles, potatoes, cèpes, sweetbreads. But with Joël Robuchon's choice of other ingredients – scallops, chestnuts, almonds, caviar – one begins to understand the uniqueness of his cuisine and philosophy.

First, they are ingredients that represent the different regions of France – truffles from Périgord, cèpes from Bordeaux, etc. Second, they are products that represent the different seasons of the year – autumn cèpes, springtime scallops and, of course, the product that created his reputation, the potato! But there are also a variety of products that, when manipulated with French techniques and a profound understanding of tastes and flavors, come alive, such as the one non-French product here: caviar from the Caspian sea.

In choosing his palette of ingredients, so to speak, Robuchon was also looking for

"products that everyone may have heard about, but do not know how to use properly, or to their maximum."

Here, then, is a visit, product by product, with an inside look at Robuchon's attachment to each one, his influence over it, and a glance at the growers who bring the products to his doorstep.

● THE NOBLEST OF VEGETABLES

"You can't judge a chef by his most complex and elaborate dishes, but by the most banal!" Robuchon announces with an almost triumphant aire. And he has the right to say so. After all, it was chef Robuchon who brought the potato to new gastronomic heights with his famed "potato puree."

In truth, save for its place as an omnipresent bistro garnish – usually boiled or as part of the sacred steak-frites (French Fries) ritual – few chefs took the potato seriously.

Today, what restaurant of any stature, any level – from the grandest tables to the simplest bistros – has not tried to copy Robuchon's simple, sublime, smooth, buttery, ecstasy-provoking "Purée de pommes de terre?"

The potato challenged him for many reasons. It's world-wide popularity, for one. Next to pasta, the potato is the Western world's preferred starch, the one food that recalls a flood of childhood taste memories for almost all of us. Not surprisingly, of all his suppliers, it is with a simple potato farmer that Robuchon has the best rapport. In fact, the success of Robuchon's puree and the subsequent publicity given to that potato's grower – Jean-Pierre Clot of Villegagnon, to the east of Paris – turned the outgoing potato farmer into a world superstar farmer. "Robuchon changed my life," says Clot. Not only have journalists from around the world flocked to his farm in hopes of capturing the secret of the now famed "ratte" potato puree, but farmers from as far away as Oregon have come to gather samples of his clay and lime-

rich soil, in hopes of duplicating the tiny, uniform, buttery potato at home. It was in 1986 that Clot was encouraged to bring samples of his ratte potato to the top chefs of Paris.

Joël Robuchon accepted, and soon he was making regular visits to Jamin's kitchen, with his 25-pound sacks of smooth-skinned rattes. Clot laughs about all the chefs who call him in confusion, saying they're doing everything Robuchon does with their own puree, but it doesn't resemble the master's. "Most chefs are simply too lazy to pass that puree through the sieve one more time. That makes all the difference between a good chef and a great chef."

● PEARLS FROM THE SEA

Caviar is one of the world's most elegant products: its glistening, jewel-like, translucent little eggs are like pearls from the

Jean-Pierre Clot, from Villega-gnon to the east of Paris, was a simple potato producer until the day he became Joël Robuchon's supplier. The success of the famous puree has given him star status in the world of agriculture.

sea, while its lingering aftertaste – like a breath of clean, salty sea water on the palate – has connoisseurs coming back for more. Yet like many of the most noble ingredients, it is elusive, as well as highly misunderstood.

"I love caviar for its strong flavor a bit of saltiness, a bit of bitterness, a bit of iodine essence of the sea, even a touch of sweet-ness, and of course, acidity. When you think of it, caviar exhibits, all by itself, all the qualities that are indispensable to a dish!" Robuchon's love affair with caviar in the kitchen began, like so many of his loves, as a self challenge. His goal was to create a dish that best married the unctuous, creamy qualities of sour cream with the complex nature of caviar.

As with many ingredients, Robuchon does not denature the caviar, or attempt to mask any of its gustative or textural qualities in his cuisine. It is in a way surprising to note that even though caviar is one of the products that helped build Robuchon's reputation – his "Gelée de caviar à la crème de chou-fleur" is perhaps his most famous dish – it is in fact not a cooked ingredient.

"For me, a good caviar is one that has an agreeable texture, not the least bit glue-like or soft," explains Robuchon, who goes on to say that the other qualities he insists upon from suppliers include grains that are whole and sparkling and detach well, and eggs that are not too white – for he knows by experience that they will inevitably be less tasty.

● A PURITY OF TASTE

Like all of today's caviar, Robuchon's comes from the Caspian sea where, each spring and each autumn, fishing boats set out to capture the precious sturgeon. Each type of caviar is described by the size of sturgeon from which it comes. The most expensive variety on the market, for inst-ance, comes from the largest variety of sturgeon, the Beluga.

The Oscetra variety of sturgeon – the variety Robuchon uses in his kitchen – is considerably smaller than the Beluga, usually weighing in at about 80 kilos per fish. The eggs also vary greatly in color. Though occasionally gray or black, they are more commonly brownish-yellow.

Though less expensive than the Beluga, the hint of iodine is more pronounced, with overtones that recall the freshness of sea air. Robuchon also professes a personal love for pressed caviar, with its very condensed, intense, jam-like quality. Pressed caviar is prepared with eggs that are crushed or compacted. The intensity comes from the fact that it takes four kilos of crushed eggs to produce one kilo of pressed caviar. Thus, what one loses in texture and looks, one gains in intensity of flavor.

Strong flavors characterize another product of the sea, the coquille Saint-Jacques or scallop. "Talk to the men who fish for scallops. What do they prefer to eat? They prefer the taste of the scallop without the coral, for its flavor is more intense than the scallop with the coral. Yes, the coral is beautiful, but while the coral is growing it saps the energy from the scallop, dilutes its naturally sweet flavor and softens the flesh." Joël Robuchon does not follow fashion, he creates it. Such is the case with a dish he invented in 1994 for the opening of his new restaurant on Avenue Raymond-Poincaré, "Noix de Saint-Jacques cuites en coquilles aux aromates" (Scallops roasted in their shells with herbs and butter), a dish of unadorned simplicity that seeks to bring out the pure, natural sweetness of the scallop. For many years, it has been the mode in France to prefer scallops with their coral, the bright, shiny, tiny orange-colored roe that represents the female of this hermaphrodite mollusk.

But, as with all ingredients, Robuchon ignored common wisdom and went to the source, researching the manner and flavor of the scallop, seeking to preserve as deep and natural a flavor as possible.

● **DIRECT FROM THE BRITTANY COASTS**

Examine the scallops that come into Robuchon's kitchens – supplied for the past ten years by Francois Gallen and his family – and you will see the Breton mollusk at its best: firm, pearly-white and translucent. As the two striated shells are opened, the flesh trembles and pulsates, it almost seems to inhale and exhale. His scallops are cleaned rapidly under cold water to remove any excess sand. They are in fact treated like mushrooms: scallops must never be allowed to soak in water – in 15 minutes they will absorb up to half their weight!

● **PRESERVING NATURAL FLAVORS**

With its delicate, slightly sweet flavor, the scallop lends itself easily to several preparations and garnishes. Avoid overpowering spices and herbs, as they can mask the delicate taste of the flesh. Even more important is the cooking time – cook the scallops briefly and at the last minute, just before sitting down to eat.

Chef Robuchon confesses that he selected the scallop as one of his eight essential products more for the cooking method that the characteristics of the product itself. After much reflection, Robuchon decided that the best way to cook scallops was to cook them

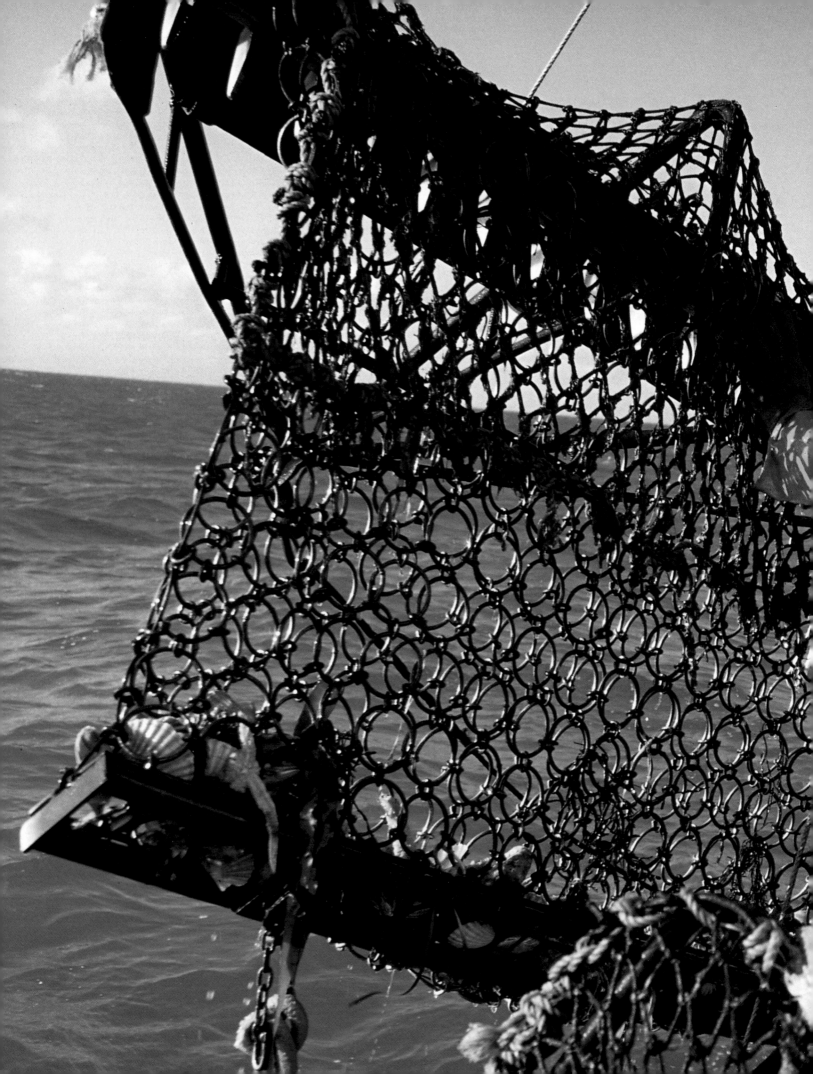

in the same way as fish, shellfish, poultry, or meat – whole and on the bone. There is less loss of flavor, better texture and form, and no loss of moistness when they are cooked in this way."

It seemed that the most logical way to cook the scallop was not just in its shell, but still attached to the shell, as one cooks meat on the bone. Why try to do better than nature? Cooking in its shell makes for the most flavorful scallop, and best of all, it keeps the ingredient the closest to its natural state."

● A TASTE OF CHILDHOOD

For Robuchon the wild cèpe represents a pure, Proustian taste of childhood. "When I was young, we had so many cèpes that we practically threw them away! We ate them all the time. The cèpe was considered a vegetable to feed the poor."

With its brown hat and clean white flesh, the cèpe is actually a member of the boletus family of mushrooms. While there are some sixty-five varieties of boletus, only a few of them – such as the prized cèpe of Bordeaux, the "bronzed cèpe" and the darker, almost black, "tête de nègre" – fall under the appellation "cèpe."

If Robuchon chose the cèpe as one of his eight essential products it's because he considers it one of France's finest native products – an ingredient that is instantly associated with France and French cuisine.

At Jamin, his "Veal chop with wild mushrooms" became a Robuchon classic. But in the 1990's he felt a need to go beyond traditional treatments this favorite ingredient. After what he describes as a period of trial and error, with many false

starts, he came up with a dish he feels exploits and respects the essence of the wild mushroom: "Cèpes grillés au thym et caviar d'aubergine." (Grilled wild mushrooms with thyme and eggplant caviar.) To his palate, the ingredients share a nuttiness as well as an elusive, slightly smoky flavor.

His goal here, as always, was to exploit the cèpe's greatest qualities: its musky taste, slightly reminiscent of hazelnuts, its firm and mildly perfumed flesh, and a meat that relaxes as it cooks, much like eggplant!

● A NOBLE SIMPLICITY

What do Robuchon and his chefs look for in a wild mushroom? Naturally, the best cèpes are those that are fresh and relatively small in size. Consume them soon after their purchase. Above all, advises the chef, avoid keeping them piled on top of one another in the refrigerator, or they are sure to begin rotting from excess moisture. To clean them, avoid rinsing them, unless they are heavily covered with dirt. Instead, wipe them with a clean damp cloth. With the tip of a small knife, remove the hard flesh at the bottom of the stem and brush away any excess dirt. If the flesh of the stems is soft, watery or wormy, remove it as well, it can radically alter the taste of the other elements in a dish. If the flesh on the underside of the cap is green or particularly soft, use the tip of the knife to gently scrape it off. Obviously, there are many ways to appreciate the cèpe. Try many types of cooking method. Add a few drops of olive oil, or goose or duck fat. "Try them with a touch of walnut oil," advises Robuchon, "as we do in my native region of Poitou."

● TRADITION AND INNOVATION

As defender of traditional French cuisine, Robuchon chose sweetbreads – one of the most frequently consumed organ meats in France – as one of his essential products. The chef also selected sweetbreads because he loves them – loves to eat them and loves to prepare them in any number of ways.

Like a painter's blank canvas, sweetbreads serve almost as a neutral, delicately flavored and finely textured backdrop, on which one can contrast many additional textures and flavors, from wild morel mushrooms to the earthy, mysterious black truffle, as in his delectable, wildly modern and creative "Ris de veau aux truffes et tiges de romaine."

Benoît Guichard, Joël Robuchon's chef, begins by soaking the whole sweetbread in cold water. While some recommend a twenty-four hour soak, Robuchon considers four to five hours ideal. The water must be changed often, until it is totally clear of blood. Next, sweetbreads must be blanched to facilitate the removal of the outer membrane and connective tissues that surround the flesh. Blanching – ideally, about four minutes – also gives the sweetbreads a more solid form without cooking them completely. Once properly blanched, they can easily be sliced into escalopes for frying or poaching.

Traditionally, sweetbreads have been wrapped in a clean towel and covered with a heavy weight to press them into a compact shape for cooking. Yet both chefs contend that if a cook has done his work properly, has carefully soaking and blanching the sweetbreads – the sweetbreads will hold their form without any need for further handling. They will have a fresher flavor.

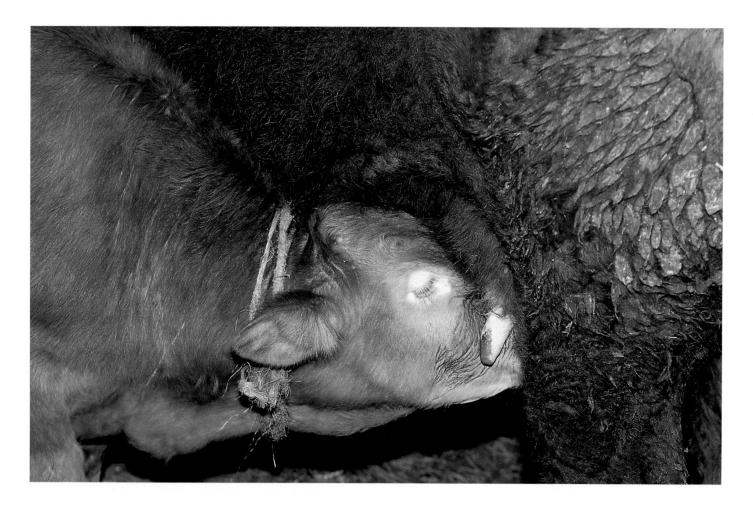

● AN ATTENTIVE SELECTION

Technically speaking, sweetbreads are the thymus gland (located near the throat) and the pancreas (located near the stomach) of calves and lambs.

The best tasting sweetbreads come from the young animal, for as the animal's diet shifts from mother's milk to other foods, the organs toughen.

Selecting sweetbreads is not an easy task, as even Robuchon's friend and veal supplier, Robert Fabre, a renowned butcher in Aurillac confirms.

"In most cases, the thymus and pancreas are sold together and are distinguishable by their shape: the pancreas is a round morsel (la noix), prized for its buttery flavor and compact flesh, while the thymus is irregular and elongated."

"Ideally, the best sweetbreads are the largest and the whitest, but looking only for those characteristics can get the consumer in trouble," Fabre admits. He advises consumers to avoid any pieces with dark discoloration.

The outer skin should show signs of moisture: if it is not shiny and glistening, this is a sign that the sweetbreads are not fresh.

Likewise, fresh sweetbreads will have firm, outer membrane with no trouble holding its compact shape.

Like all organ meats, sweetbreads deteriorate rapidly, and they should be prepared as soon after they are purchased as possible.

● A PRUDENT EXPLORATION
   WITH AUDACIOUS MARRIAGES

"I first tasted a fresh truffle at the age of 18, as an apprentice," Robuchon recalls. "It was a shock. I was surprised by its perfume and its texture, two seemingly obvious qualities that are completely lost when a truffle is preserved."

But revolutions do not happen overnight. And it took a rare chef to gradually transform one of the world's finest gastronomic jewels from a decorative trinket into a noble product worthy of serious gastronomic exploration.

When Joël Robuchon was finally on his own, at Jamin, he began exploring and exploiting those fresh truffle qualities. He began slowly, almost timidly, with his first truffle menu in December 1981 menu that included a "Sauté prawns, braised sweetbreads and vegetables with truffles," and "Scallops with truffles and artichokes." One can see that even then he was exploring uncommon alliances: artichokes and truffles as partners from the earth, and langoustines and truffles as earth-sea companions. Even his first all-truffle menu – with two simple truffle dishes, one of which was the forerunner of his now legendary truffle tart – appears timid when compared to his wholloping, wildly creative menus of the 1990s, when he paired truffles with the sweet-nutty flavors of fresh white beans, or coco blancs, and created an almost mystical

It is thanks to Jacques Peybere and his son Pierre-Jean, whose "insatiable curiosity and obsession with detail" is celebrated by Robuchon, that the truffle has taken on a new importance in the palette of ingredients he has made his own. By working with the Peyberes, the world's greatest experts on and suppliers of truffles, Robuchon has succeeded in revealing the hidden essence of the famous tuber.

salad that included fresh raw truffles bathed in a celery vinaigrette.

When Joël Robuchon offered an all-truffle menu at Jamin in 1981, he began changing the way France – and the world – looked at the rare, black "tuber melanosporum." He was among the first chefs to treat the famed, earthy truffle as the principle flavor ingredient, not simply a snobbish garnish.

"Thanks to Robuchon's intense need to know everything about a product, he has learned to draw the maximum from a truffle, to discover at what temperature it cooks best, even what happens when the truffle is sliced, diced, minced or simply cooked whole," explains Jacques Peybere.

● THE SUMPTUOUSNESS OF A SURPRISE

Yes, the black truffle that lives symbiotically with certain oak and hazelnut trees has been revered for centuries as one of France's gastronomic treasures.

Yet until Robuchon turned his acutely focused attention to this mysterious mushroom unearthed, in northern Provence and the Périgord, few had truly worked to draw out the truffle's maximum aroma, to examine its texture and to begin to create a roster of soon-to-be-classic truffle pairings.

"Truffles are really all about texture – that crunch, that element of surprise," says Robuchon. "For me," he says with a certain containment at the end of his restaurant career, "the truffle is totally, 100 percent French. It is the ingredient that has most

influenced my cooking, and the one that has been most appreciated by my clients." Robuchon's challenge was to take an already revered ingredient and make it sublime.

"And the difference between good and sublime," explains Joël Robuchon,"is not a negligible, it is a enormous."

● A FRUIT WORTH REDISCOVERING

Much like the prized cèpe mushrooms, the chestnut was chosen by chef Robuchon for its intense Proustian properties.

"In my childhood, chestnuts were plentiful, they were available to everyone, the rich and the poor." It is this commonplace side of the ubiquitous chestnut that attracts Joël Robuchon, as well as its standing as a typically French product.

The chef has put his own stamp on the treatment of the chestnut by pairing it with the noble lobster – as in his "Lobster baked with truffles and chestnuts." To test for freshness, slice the chestnut in half, peel away a small section of outer skin and examine the flesh: it should be "as fresh as the flesh of a potato that has just been sliced."

● A SUBTLE PREPARATION

But no matter how beautiful the chestnut is, the secret to drawing out and capturing its nutty essence is cooking it properly. Take the example of the chestnut that forms the base of a rich and warming wintry confit of whole chestnuts, fennel, walnuts and onions – all bathed in a dose of newly pressed walnut oil from France's southwest region.

The chestnuts are first carefully pierced, by means of a gentle incision down the length of each nut. This allows the nut to release its moisture as it cooks, swelling slightly and making it easier to peel.

Robuchon then drops the chestnuts into a pan of hot oil, cooking them for just two or three minutes until the shells curl away from the meat, transforming the banal chestnut into a richly nutty, smooth, mouth-filling, ingredient fit for a king.

● FLAVORS WITH A SOUVENIR OF PAST TRAVELS

The choice of almonds as one of Joël Robuchon's prized products represents the final stages of his brilliant restaurant career. During the last days of Restaurant Joël Robuchon, he permitted himself to travel beyond the French borders, filling his menu with varied "plats du voyage" – dishes inspired by travels around the world.

One modern dish, the "Baby zucchini with bacon, fresh almonds and mint," represents his love affair with Moroccan cuisine, which features the sweet Mediterranean almond in both sweet as well as salty dishes.

The choice of the Mediterranean almond also represents the evolution of his cuisine – from a mainly Parisian menu in the 1980's to one in the 1990's, where such southern-inspired ingredients as tomato confit, shellfish grilled with rosemary, penne pasta, and eggplant-stuffed cannelloni seem to sing a Provençal lullaby to hover over the pages of the menu.

Robuchon's chooses the fresh, springtime almonds of Provence. The "fruit" of the tender almond tree is the first to bloom in the spring. Rich in oil as well as sugar, the fresh almonds marry perfectly with spring green-zucchini and zesty mint.

"I first tasted the combination of almonds and mint on a trip to Morocco," explains Robuchon, "and spent years trying to re-create that freshness of flavors. I feel I found it, by adding the crispy texture of the lightly fried zucchini blossom and the earthy taste of the zucchini." Joël Robuchon challenges us, once again, questioning the commonplace, moving beyond conventional borders and boundaries.

Recipes

Potato puree (Mashed Potatoes)

BY JOËL ROBUCHON

6 SERVINGS

INGREDIENTS
- **2 pounds (1 kg)
  ratte or BF15 potatoes**
- **3/4 to 1 1/4 cups (20 to 30 ml)
  whole milk, heated**
- **16 tablespoons (8 ounces; 250 g)
  unsalted butter, chilled, and cut
  into small pieces**
- **Coarse sea salt to taste**

**Secrets of Joël Robuchon's
perfect PURÉE**

**The quantity of butter and milk needed
for a successfully silken and satiny puree
will vary according to the potatoes and
the season. Early season potatoes will be
firmer, demanding more butter and milk
for a perfectly soft, almost fluffy, puree.
The key to a perfect puree is choosing
potatoes of uniform size (so they are
uniformly cooked) and a strong arm for
drying the potatoes with a flat wooden
spatula. Be sure that the butter is well
chilled, for it will help make a finer,
smoother puree. Also follow the
proportions of salt to water when
cooking the potatoes – you won't be able
to make up for it with additional salt at
the end.**

Scrub the potatoes but do not peel. Place the potatoes in a large saucepan and fill with enough cold water to cover by at least 1 inch (3 cm). For each quart (liter) of water, add 1 tablespoon (10 g) of salt. Simmer, uncovered, over moderate heat for 20 to 30 minutes until a knife inserted into a potato comes away easily.

Drain the potatoes as soon as they are cooked. (If allowed to cool in the water, the potatoes will taste re-heated.)

Meanwhile, in a large saucepan, bring the milk just to a boil over high heat. Set aside.

Once the potatoes are cool enough to handle, peel them and cut into manageable pieces. Pass the potatoes through the finest grid of a food mill into a large, heavy-bottomed saucepan.

Place the pan over low heat, and, with a wooden spatula, stir the potatoes vigorously to dry them, 4 to 5 minutes.

Now begin adding about three-quarters of the butter, little by little, stirring vigorously until each batch of butter is thoroughly incorporated and the mixture becomes fluffy and light.

Slowly add about three-quarters of the hot milk in a thin stream, stirring vigorously, until the milk is thoroughly incorporated.

● Cook the potatoes in their skins.

● Pass the potatoes through the finest grid of a food mill.

● Incorporate the cold butter in cubes.

● Slowly add the hot milk in a thin, continuous stream.

For an extra-fine puree, pass the mixture through a drum sieve into another heavy-bottomed saucepan.

Place over low heat and stir vigorously. If the puree seems a bit heavy and stiff, add additional butter and milk, whisking all the while.

Taste for seasoning. (The puree may be prepared up to 1 hour in advance. Place in the top of a double boiler over gently simmering water. Whisk occasionally to keep smooth.)

Wine suggestion: serve with a roussette-de-Savoie, a tasty white known for its perfume of white fruits and summer flowers.

● Stir vigorously until all of the milk is thoroughly incorporated.

● Stir the puree with a whisk to make it fluffy.

● Pass the puree through a drum sieve to make it extra-fine and light.

● Use a spoon to smooth the surface of the puree.

“ WHAT OTHER VEGETABLE MANAGES TO ACCOMPANY SO MANY DIVERSE DISHES, ALWAYS OFFERING SUCH PERFECT SUBTLETY? AN INGREDIENT APPRECIATED BY EVERYONE, IN EVERY SEASON. ”

SUMMARY

● Joël Robuchon ●

A potato puree – simple and elegant – a dish that pleases people of all ages. Joel Robuchon's "Purée de Pommes de Terre," found on the very first menu at Jamin in 1981, reveals one of the best aspects of his culinary success. A recipe that pays homage to the products of France, namely the "ratte" variety of potato, with the perfection of a master.

● Dominique Bouchet ●

Dominique Bouchet has retained the importance of simplicity in this potato dish. His famous "Pommes Gueulantes," which combines four basic ingredients – butter, fresh thyme, salt and potatoes – for a tasty and appealing dish. Cooked slowly over a low heat for a minimum of two hours, the result is potatoes bathed in the tastes of the earth.

● Christophe Cussac ●

Christophe Cussac, taking his inspiration from his master's dish, creates a gratin of potato puree with a touch of the region of Burgundy. His "Crème de pommes de terre au Chaource" blends the elements of a puree – milk, butter, cream – with Chaource – a cow's milk cheese from the Aube.

● Benoît Guichard ●

Operating on a similar principle to Christophe Cussac, Benoît Guichard's "Gratin de pommes de terre" layers potato and Reblochon cheese rounds on a bed of bacon and onions. A rustic potato dish reminiscent of the Savoyard classic "Tartiflette de Reblochon," in which onions and potato are combined with Reblochon cheese.

● Philippe Groult ●

Philippe Groult creates a dish centered around a potato puree, but he has retained an important lesson from his master: the difference is in the details. His "Brandade de petits rougets" combines potato puree and pan-seared filets of red mullet. The addition of fried croutons for texture, and celery leaves for a bright, shocking color, results in a dish with many different elements of taste and texture.

● Maurice Guillouët ●

Maurice Guillouët bridges the gap between the tastes of the earth – potato – and those of the sea – lobster. His "Fricassée de homard aux pommes de terre" is a simple but flavorful sauté of potatoes and lobster perfumed with dill and garlic. Opting similarly for the "ratte" variety of potato, Guillouet's intelligent marriage of two noble products reveals his fidelity, even as chef in a kitchen as far away as Tokyo, Japan, to the ingredients and elegance of France.

Potatoes sautéed in butter with thyme

BY DOMINIQUE BOUCHET

Peel the potatoes. With a sharp, medium-size knife, shape each potato into a rectangle 3 inches (7 1/2 cm) long, and 2 inches (5 cm) wide. Cut each rectangle evenly in half lengthwise to obtain 2 slices of the same thickness. The 6 potatoes should yield a total of 12 slices.

With a small sharp knife, shape each slice into an oval 2 inches (5 cm) long and 1 1/2 inches (3.75 cm) wide.

Rinse the potatoes. Prepare a large bowl of ice water.
Place the potatoes in a saucepan. Cover generously with cold water and season using 1 tablespoon salt per quart (liter) water. Bring to the boil over high heat. As soon as the water boils drain the potatoes and plunge them into the ice water so they cool down as quickly as possible.

Place the potatoes, then the butter, in a large skillet (preferably copper). Adjust heat to the lowest possible setting. Season to taste.

Cook for one hour without turning them, basting every 5 to 6 minutes with the butter as they cook. Turn the potatoes and cook for an additional hour, basting them with the butter every 5 to 6 minutes. The potatoes should be golden brown with a slightly crispy outer skin.

Remove and with a fork, gently press down on each potato to remove excess butter before serving.

To serve, arrange six potatoes like petals of a daisy in the center of a warmed dinner plate. Place a tiny bouquet of fresh thyme in the center. Repeat for the remaining serving. Serve immediately.

2 SERVINGS

- 6 large potatoes, such as Charlotte, each weighing about 8 ounces (250g)
- 19 tablespoons (295 g) clarified butter
- Fine sea salt to taste
- 2 bouquets of fresh thyme

Wine suggestion: a light and tasty white from the Jura, such as an Arbois.

Potatoe puree with Chaource cheese

BY CHRISTOPHE CUSSAC

Preheat the oven to 450° F (230° C; gas mark 9).

Place the potatoes in the center of the oven and roast until a fork inserted into a potato comes away easily, 15 to 20 minutes.

As soon as the potatoes are cool enough to handle, peel them. Pass through the finest grid of the food mill over a large bowl. Add the cheese, 4 (90 g) egg yolks, 1 1/4 cups (30 cl) heavy cream and the milk. With a wooden spatula, stir the potatoes to blend. Taste for seasoning.

Preheat the oven to the lowest setting possible. Butter the gratin dishes and fill with the potato mixture. Place in the center of the oven and cook for 30 minutes.

Remove and set aside to cool for about 30 minutes.

Preheat the broiler. With a brush, coat the potatoes with the remaining egg yolk. Place them under the broiler until golden brown.

Place the remaining 3/4 cup (20 cl) cream in a small saucepan. Season lightly and reduce over a low heat, 8 to 10 minutes. Add the minced chives. Taste for seasoning. Set aside.

To serve: place each gratin dish on a warm dinner plate. Sprinkle the potatoes with Sel de Guérande and nutmeg. Pour the remaining sauce into a warmed sauceboat and serve alongside.

6 SERVINGS

- 2 to 3 (400 g) "Charlotte" potatoes, washed
- 1/3 pound (150 g) Chaource cheese
- 5 (120 g) egg yolks, 1 reserved for the egg glaze
- 2 cups (50 cl) heavy cream
- 6 tablespoons (10 cl) whole milk
- 1 tablespoon (15 g) butter
- Sea salt and freshly ground white pepper to taste
- 2 tablespoons finely minced fresh chives
- Sel de Guérande, for final seasoning
- Freshly grated nutmeg to taste

SPECIAL MATERIAL

- 6 porcelain gratin dishes, 6 inches (15 cm) in diameter

Wine suggestion: a white coteau champenois.

Brandade of Baby Red Mullet

BY PHILIPPE GROULT

Prepare the red mullet: in a pan large enough to hold the fillets in a single layer, sprinkle half of the minced garlic and the thyme. Place the red mullet fillets skin up and cover with 11 tablespoons of the olive oil. Refrigerate to infuse for 3 hours.

Prepare the fish stock: in a medium saucepan, combine the remaining olive oil and fennel. Cook until softened, about 5 minutes. Add the fish bones and heads, increase the heat to high, and cook for 3 minutes more. Add the water, a pinch of coarse sea salt and simmer for 7 minutes, skimming off any impurities that rise to the top.

Line a sieve with a moistened cheesecloth and set over a medium-size bowl. Ladle (do not pour) the stock into the prepared sieve.
Rinse the saucepan and return the strained stock to the pan. Reduce over high heat until syrupy, 10 to 15 minutes. Set aside.

Cook the potatoes: place the unpeeled potatoes in a large pot, add salted water (1 tablespoon salt per quart of water) to cover by at least 1 inch. Simmer, uncovered, over moderate heat until a knife in-serted into a potato comes away easily, 20 to 30 minutes. Drain the potatoes as soon as they are cooked. Peel them and set aside.

Prepare the heart-shaped croutons: heat a medium-size skillet until hot, but not smoking. Add 2 tablespoons clarified butter fol-lowed by half of the heart-shaped slices of bread. Fry quickly over medium-high heat until golden brown on both sides, 2 to 3 minutes. Season lightly with salt and pepper. Remove. Drain on paper towels. Repeat for the remaining croutons, using fresh butter for the second batch. Set aside.

Prepare the garnish: in a small skillet, heat 1 tablespoon clarified butter until hot, but not smoking. Add the petals of garlic and brown lightly over moderate heat, 1 minute. Take care not to burn them. Season lightly with salt and pepper. Drain. Set aside.

Pour the peanut oil into a heavy-bottomed saucepan, or use a deep-fat fryer. Heat the oil to 350° F (175° C). Fry the celery leaves in batches (about 6 leaves at a time,) until crispy and trans-lucent, 1 to 2 minutes. With a flat-mesh skimmer, transfer to paper towels to drain. Sprinkle immediately with salt. Set aside.

Preheat the oven to 275° F (135° C; gas mark 2). Cook the red mullet: arrange the red mullet fillets in a single layer in an oven-proof pan. Reserve the marinade separately. Place the pan in the center of the oven and cook for 2 minutes. Remove and set aside.

Prepare the potatoes: In a large, heavy-bottomed saucepan, crush the potatoes one by one with a fork. With a wooden spatula, stir the potatoes vigorously to dry them out. Add a few tablespoons of the red mullet marinade and the remaining chopped garlic and the chopped parsley. Mix to blend.

Finish the potatoes: in a small bowl, crush 6 red mullet fillets with a fork. Add them to the potato puree. Blend in the reduced fish stock and the crème fraîche. Taste for seasoning. To serve: spoon the puree into 4 warmed, shallow soup bowls. Arrange 5 small fillets in a circle in the center on top of the puree. Arrange 3 petals of garlic around the fillets as well as a few leaves of dried celery. Finish with the heart-shaped croutons around the edges. Serve immediately.

4 SERVINGS

THE RED MULLET

- 4 plump, fresh, garlic cloves, peeled and minced
- 1 small bunch fresh thyme, washed
- 26 small red mullet fillets, scaled and deboned
- 12 tablespoons (18.5 cl) extra-virgin olive oil

FOR THE FISH STOCK

- 1/2 bulb fennel, chopped
- 13 cleaned fish skeletons (bones and heads), well-rinsed and cut up
- 1/2 cup (12.5 cl) water
- Coarse salt

FOR THE PUREE

- 2 pounds (1 kg) yellow-fleshed potatoes, such as Charlotte, scrubbed
- 1 small bunch fresh flat-leaf parsley, washed and chopped
- 4 tablespoons (6 cl) crème fraîche

TO FINISH

- 5 tablespoons (2 1/2 ounces; 75 g) clarified butter
- 20 heart-shaped pieces of white bread, cut with a small cookie cutter
- 2 garlic cloves, peeled, each cut into 6 thin slices
- 1 quart (1 liter) peanut oil, for frying
- 20 small, yellow celery leaves from the heart of the celery, washed and dried

Wine suggestion: a Bandol Rosé from Provence.

Individual potato gratin

BY BENOÎT GUICHARD

Peel and wash the potatoes. In a large stockpot, combine the potatoes, pot-au-feu bouillon, unpeeled garlic, and sprigs of thyme. Simmer over moderate heat until the potatoes are cooked but still firm, 15 to 20 minutes. (Do not boil the potatoes or they will fail to hold their shape).

Drain, reserving the cooking liquid. Cut the potatoes into even, 1/4-inch (5 mm) slices. Set aside.

In a small saucepan, combine 1 tablespoon butter, the onions and minced garlic. Cover, and sweat over moderate heat until soft, about 15 minutes. Set aside.

If the bacon is salty, bring 2 cups (50 cl) water to a rolling boil. Add the bacon and blanch for 1 minute, counting from the time the water returns to a boil. Drain. Refresh in cold water. In a large skillet, combine the peanut oil and the bacon. Color lightly over moderate heat, 2 to 3 minutes. Add the onions and white wine, and cook to blend the flavors, about 2 minutes. Add a small ladle of pot-au-feu bouillon.

Cover and cook over a low heat until all the liquid has been reduced, about 15 minutes. Set aside.

Preheat the oven to 400° F (200° C; gas mark 6/7). Evenly divide the onion and bacon compote among 4 round, oven-proof gratin dishes. Even out with the back of a spoon. Arrange overlapping, alternating slices of potato and cheese in clockwise circles on top of the compote. Garnish with thyme leaves and coarsely ground white pepper.

Place the gratin dishes in the center of the oven and bake until the potatoes are firm and the gratin is bubbling, about 15 minutes. Serve immediately, as an accompaniment to a roast meat or poultry.

4 SERVINGS

- 12 small, firm, yellow-fleshed potatoes (BF 15), each about the size of an egg, peeled and washed
- 1 quart (1 l) pot-au-feu bouillon (or substitute veal or poultry stock)
- 3 plump, fresh garlic cloves, unpeeled
- 2 sprigs fresh thyme
- 3 tablespoons (50 g; 2 oz) plus 1 teaspoon unsalted butter
- 12 spring onions, peeled and finely chopped
- 1 plump, fresh garlic clove, minced
- 10 ounces (300 g) lightly smoked bacon, diced
- 2 tablespoons (12 cl) peanut oil
- 3 tablespoons (18 cl) white wine
- Half a Reblochon cheese
- Fresh thyme leaves and flowers, for garnish
- Coarsely ground white pepper to taste

SPECIAL MATERIAL

- 1 round cutter, 1 inch (2.5 cm) in diameter
- 4 small, oven-proof porcelain dishes 6 inches (15 cm) wide

Wine suggestion: a white coteau champenois.

Fricassee of Lobster with Potatoes

BY MAURICE GUILLOUËT

Prepare the lobster: in a large pot, bring 6 quarts (6 l) water to a rolling boil. With scissors, remove the rubber bands restraining the claws, and plunge the lobster head first into the water. Counting from the time the lobster hits the water, cook for 3 minutes. (The lobsters may be cooked one at a time.) Remove and drain.

Remove the meat from the lobster: twist each large claw off the body of the lobster. Gently crack the claw shells with a nutcracker or a hammer, trying not to damage the meat. Extract the meat with a seafood fork; it should come out in a single piece. Set aside. Gently detach the tail from the rest of the body and place it on a flat work surface. With a long sharp knife, cut the lobster tail crosswise into 4 equal parts. With a small knife, remove the thin intestinal tract found in the lower segment of the tail meat. Discard. Set aside the tail pieces.

Remove and reserve the dark green coral, if it is present, from the head and the upper portion of the body cavity. Set aside.

Prepare the sauce: in a large saucepan, heat the olive oil until it smokes lightly. Add the lobster shells and sear, tossing constantly, for 1 to 2 minutes. Add the shallot and fennel and cook for an additional 2 minutes, mixing from time to time. Add the water and fennel seeds. Season to taste. Cover and simmer over moderate heat, 10 minutes. Remove from heat and allow to cool for at least 15 minutes. Pass through a fine-mesh seive into another casserole and reduce to half. Set aside.

Prepare the potato garnish: in a medium-size skillet, heat 3 tablespoons (45 g) butter over moderate heat. Add the garlic cloves and the potatoes and cook, covered, for 8 to 10 minutes. Taste for seasoning. Drain and set aside.

Cook the lobster: in a medium-size skillet, heat 3 tablespoons (45 g) butter over moderate heat. Season the tail meat with salt and pepper and cook for 3 minutes, turning once. Add the claws and the potatoes and cook for an additional 3 to 5 minutes.

Finish the sauce: heat a small saucepan over high heat and combine the remaining butter and lobster coral, whisking constantly, for 30 seconds. Whisk in the lobster sauce. Taste for seasoning.

To serve: dress the pieces of lobster and the potatoes on warmed dinner plates. Spoon the sauce over the lobster. Sprinkle with fresh dill. Serve immediately.

4 SERVINGS

- Four 1pound (500 g) lobsters, preferably female, rinsed

THE SAUCE

- 4 tablespoons (6 cl) extra-virgin olive oil
- 1 shallot, peeled and chopped
- 1/2 bulb fresh fennel, washed and chopped
- 3/4 cup (18.5 cl) water
- 1/4 teaspoon fennel seeds
- Fine sea salt
- Freshly ground pepper

GARNISH

- 10 tablespoons (5 ounces; 150 g) unsalted butter
- 2 plump, fresh garlic cloves, peeled
- 3/4 pound (375 g) small yellow-fleshed potatoes, such as "ratte," par-boiled and peeled

TO FINISH

- 2 sprigs fresh dill
- Coarse sea salt

Wine suggestion: a grand white Burgundy

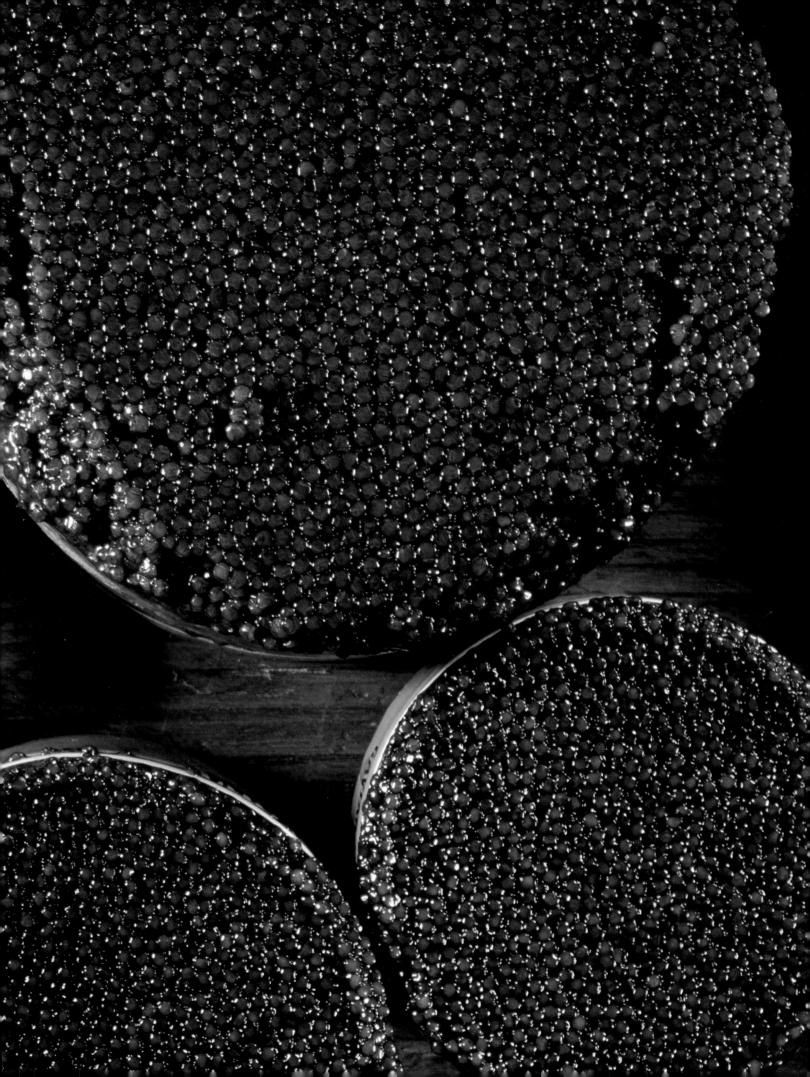

Lobster Aspic and Caviar with Cauliflower Cream

BY JOËL ROBUCHON

4 SERVINGS

INGREDIENTS
Yield: About 2 quarts (2 l) jelly
- 1 calf's foot
- Coarse sea salt

Calf's foot jelly

Calf's foot is valued for the rich-flavored, nourishing gelatin obtained when simmered for several hours in water. The gelatin enriches and enhances the texture and flavor of stews and stocks. Prepare the calf's foot: when purchased, a calf's foot generally includes the hoof and a thin upper-leg bone enclosed with flesh and skin. To prepare, split in half. With a sharp boning knife, carve away the meat and skin from the upper-leg bone. Reserve all the pieces, including the bone (or ask your butcher to do this for you).

Place the pieces in a large stockpot and add cold water to cover. Salt and bring to the boil over high heat. Simmer for 2 minutes. Drain. Return the pieces to the stockpot, place in the sink and rinse under cold running water for 15 minutes to refresh. Drain.

Clean the stockpot and combine the blanched calf's foot pieces, 2 tablespoons (30 g) salt and 4 quarts (4 l) cold water. Bring to a boil over moderately high heat. Reduce the heat to low and simmer very gently for 3 hours, skimming away any impurities that may rise to the surface.

Line a sieve with moistened cheesecloth, set the sieve over a large bowl, and ladle – do not pour – the stock into the prepared sieve. Remove the meat and gelatin from the bones. Discard the bone. Cut or pull the meat and gelatin into small pieces. Discard any hard or very firm portions of meat, gristle, or tendon. Cool at room temperature. Once cooled, transfer the jelly to a sealed container. Do the same with the chopped meaty portions. The jelly may be held refrigerated for 2 to 3 days, or frozen for up to 1 month

Cream of cauliflower

Prepare the cauliflower: break into bite-size flowerettes. Bring a large pot of water to a boil over high heat. Salt, add the cauliflower and blanch for 2 minutes. Drain and refresh under cold running water. In a large saucepan, warm the stock over moderate heat. Taste for seasoning. Add the cauliflower, cover, and simmer for 20 minutes. Place a fine-mesh sieve over a clean saucepan. Pass the cauliflower and stock through the sieve, pushing down to extract as much liquid as possible. Place the saucepan over moderate heat and cook until reduced to 2 cups (50 cl). Dissolve the cornstarch in 1 tablespoon cold water. Set aside. In a medium-size bowl, combine the egg yolk and 2/3 cup (15 cl) of the cream and whisk to blend thoroughly. Set aside.

Bring the cauliflower and stock mixture to a boil over high heat. Add the dissolved cornstarch and whisk constantly until the mixture returns to a boil. Continue whisking and allow to boil for 1 minute. Pour a little of the boiling liquid into the bowl with the cream mixture and whisk vigorously. Return the mixture to the saucepan. Place over low heat and cook, stirring constantly with a wooden spoon, until the mixture thickens to a creamy consistency. The mixture should not boil. To test, run your finger down the back of the spoon: if the mixture is sufficiently cooked, the line will hold. The whole process should take about 5 minutes. Remove from the heat.

For hot soup: add the remaining 6 tablespoons (6 cl) cream and transfer immediately to a food processor or blender to aerate the soup and make it foamy. Pour the soup into warmed, shallow soup bowls. Serve immediately.

For cold soup or caviar jelly: increase the cornstarch to 2 1/2 tablespoons (30 g). Thoroughly cool the mixture before whisking in the remaining cream.

INGREDIENTS
- 2 pounds (1 kg) cauliflower
- Sea salt to taste
- 4 cups (1 l) chicken stock, preferably homemade
- A pinch of curry
- 1 1/2 tablespoons (15 g) cornstarch
- 1 large egg yolk
- 1 cup (25 cl) heavy cream

● Cover the pieces of calf's foot with cold water, bring to a boil and simmer for 2 minutes.

● Blanch the cauliflower for 2 minutes. Drain and refresh under cold running water.

● Cook the cauliflower in 1 quart (1 l) of chicken stock with a pinch of curry.

● Pass the cauliflower and stock through a fine-mesh sieve, pushing down to extract as much liquid as possible.

● Dissolve the cornstarch, then prepare the egg yolk and cream mixture.

● Incorporate the cornstarch into the cauliflower and stock mixture, whisking constantly.

● Sear the lobster shells over high heat.

INGREDIENTS

Lobster Aspic

- 8 tablespoons (13 cl) extra-virgin olive oil
- 1/2 kg lobster carcasses, or substitute fresh crabs, rinsed and crushed
- 2 onions, peeled and minced
- 1 fennel bulb, chopped
- 3 celery sticks, chopped
- 2 carrots, peeled and chopped
- 6 shallots, coarsely chopped
- 20 white peppercorns
- 1 heaping tablespoon tomato paste
- Tarragon bouquet garni: several sprigs fresh tarragon, several parsley stems, celery leaves and sprigs of thyme, wrapped in the green part of a leek and securely fastened
- 2 quarts (2l) calf's foot jelly
- The reserved meaty portions of the calf's foot, chopped into small pieces

Lobster aspic and caviar with cauliflower jelly

In a large skillet, heat the oil over high heat. When the oil is very hot, almost smoking, add the lobster. The shells should sear, so shake the pan over high heat, cooking for 3 to 4 minutes.

In a separate casserole, heat 2 teaspoons of olive oil and cook the onions, fennel, celery, carrots and shallots without coloring, 5 minutes. Add the vegetables to the lobster shells. Season lightly with salt and white pepper. Mix to blend and add the tomato paste, the calf's foot jelly, the diced meat and the bouquet garni. Bring just to a boil, then reduce to a simmer. Simmer gently for 20 minutes, skimming the surface as necessary to remove scum and foam.

Pass the mixture through a fine-mesh sieve into a clean pot. Continue cooking and skimming until reduced to 2 cups (50 cl) liquid. Set aside to cool. The fat will rise to the surface as the mixture cools, making it easier to remove. (In clarifying, it is very important to degrease, otherwise the clarifi-

● Add the lobster shells to the skillet with the vegetables.

● Mix the ingredients with a wooden spoon.

● Simmer gently for 20 minutes.

● Pour the clarification mixture into the degreased lobster jelly.

cation will not take.) Prepare the clarification: place the egg white in a large bowl. Add one tablespoon of cold water and whisk to break up the white, for 30 seconds. Add the chopped leek, carrot and celery and stir to blend. Add the crushed ice. Set aside.

Return the degreased and thoroughly cooled jelly to moderate heat. As soon as it boils, transfer a ladleful of boiling jelly into the clarification mixture and stir to blend. Pour the jelly and clarification mixture back into the stockpot and stir with a wooden spoon until the mixture returns to a boil.

Stir frequently, and do not allow the egg white to stick to the bottom of the pan, or the clarification will not take. Add the star anise (just one pinch!) and simmer gently until the jelly is completely clarified. To test for clarification: poke a hole through the "raft" to see the liquid. If it does not seem clear, take up a ladleful from the bottom and pour it back over the top of the clarification crust. Repeat several times without stopping, as needed. Do not allow the mixture to boil. Cook slowly for 1 /12 hours. Let it rest for 30 minutes.

Line a fine-mesh sieve with dampened cheesecloth and place over a large bowl. Pour the clarified jelly through the prepared sieve and set aside to cool and solidify. To serve, divide the cauliflower cream evenly among the 4 bowls, pouring it over the set caviar jelly. Refrigerate until needed. To finish for presentation: reheat the jelly slightly, just to soften. Divide the caviar evenly among 4 oriental-style conical soup bowls. Place the caviar in the bottom of each bowl in a small dome. Slowly and carefully, pour the cooled but still liquid jelly on top. The jelly should be syrupy in texture and cold to the touch. Place in the refrigerator to firm, about 20 minutes. To serve, divide the cauliflower cream evenly among the 4 bowls, pouring it over the set caviar jelly. Refrigerate until needed.

Decorate the top with dots of the blended mayonnaise and chlorophyll. Place a small leaf of chervil in the center of each bowl. Serve.

Clarification
- 1 extra large egg white
- 1 tablespoon chopped leek
- 1 tablespoon chopped carrot
- 1 tablespoon chopped celery
- 4 tablespoons crushed ice
- A pinch of ground star anise

Decoration
- About 80 g Oscietra caviar
- 3/4 cup cream of cauliflower
- 1 tablespoon acid-free mayonnaise blended with chlorophyll
- Fresh chervil

CHLOROPHYLL
Combine raw spinach and/or parsley leaves, puree in food processor, press through cheesecloth, place in bain marie over simmering water. The liquid will coagulate. Skim off the top green portion, discarding the watery bottom portion. Transfer the reserved chlorophyll to a small bowl and cover with a film of oil. Combine 1/3 of the chlorophyll with 2/3 mayonnaise.

To serve: a grand Champagne.

● Test for clarification by poking a hole through the "raft."

● Place a portion of caviar in the bottom of each bowl.

● Carefully pour the jelly, which should be almost cold, over the caviar.

● Decorate the top of the cauliflower cream with the chlorophyll mayonnaise.

" ONE ASSOCIATES CAVIAR WITH OPULENCE, ELEGANCE, SIMPLICITY, AND CONVIVIALITY. IT HAS ALWAYS BEEN AN OLD COMPANION OF JOEL ROBUCHON'S. "

● Joël Robuchon ●

With the dish that made his fame, the "Gelée de caviar à la crème de chou-fleur," Joël Robuchon sets a high standard for his pupils. Served in a deep, Asian-style soup bowl, a meticulously-shaped spoonful of caviar coated with lobster jelly is topped with a fine layer of creamed cauliflower. Minuscule dots of chlorophyll around the edges adds the finishing touch. The tastes of the cauliflower and caviar are brought out by the lobster gelée, but the complexity is hidden to the eye.

● Dominique Bouchet ●

Dominique Bouchet's recipe remains the simplest of them all. His "Tarte de pommes de terre, saumon fumé et caviar" combines four earthy flavors and textures. A layer of potatoes serves as a base for the smoked salmon, cream and caviar. The potatoes, which lighten the smoked taste of the salmon, also enhance the taste of the fish. The cream mellows the saltiness of the caviar and invokees instead its delicate and natural iodine flavor.

•Christophe Cussac•

Christophe Cussac relies strongly on the example of his master with his "Coquetiers de homard aux œufs et caviar," blending lobster flesh with quail eggs and caviar, and layering the ingredients inside small, deep egg-cups. Like Robuchon, Cussac has created a dish where the flavors are tasted in several layers, separately but also as a complex whole.

•Benoît Guichard•

Guichard rhymes with caviar! Benoît Guichard's "Salade de pommes de terre au caviar et à l'oignon rouge" of Benoît Guichard succeeds in achieving a perfect balance between the salt of the caviar and the sweetness of the potato. With a few green vegetables and a few drops of vinaigrette he creates that subtle touch of acidity that achieves a very happy marriage.

•Philippe Groult•

Philippe Groult also marries caviar with a crustacean – a spider crab. In his "Araignée de mer d'Audierne, en carapace au caviar," Groult plays with the same balance of sweet crab flesh and salty caviar. The recipe is slightly different: the composition is neatly dressed in the body of the crab, giving a strong sense of connection with the crab in its natural state.

•Maurice Guillouët•

With his "Cannellonis de truite de mer," Maurice Guillouet also manages to hide the complexity of the dish. The caviar, rolled inside a thin layer of sea trout, is coated with a butter sauce lightly perfumed with fennel and onions. Fennel and onions – elements that enhance the flavor of the fish and caviar without overwhelming the dish.

Potato Tart
with Smoked Salmon and Caviar

BY DOMINIQUE BOUCHET

Prepare the potatoes: peel the potatoes, rinse under cold running water, and pat dry. Grate the potatoes with a food mill or a hand grater. Transfer to a bowl and season to taste with salt, pepper and nutmeg.

Cook the potatoes: in each of the four nonstick blini pans, heat 1 tablespoon of peanut oil over moderately high heat. When hot, fill each pan with an even 1/4 inch thick (1/2 cm) layer of grated potatoes and press with a spatula to compress.

Brown the potatoes thoroughly on one side before turning to brown the other side. Lower the heat and cook slowly until a knife inserted in the center comes away easily, cooking about 5 to 7 minutes per side. Unmold the potato cakes and transfer to prewarmed dinner plates.

To serve: carefully drape three slices of smoked salmon in a circular pattern on top of each potato cake. With a tablespoon, make a small quenelle of whipped cream for each cake and place it on top of the smoked salmon.

Place a spoonful of caviar on top of each quenelle of whipped cream. Arrange three leaves of flat-leaf parsley like a bouquet, pressing them into the base of each spoonful of caviar.

Serve immediately.

4 SERVINGS

POTATOES

- 1 pound (500 g) Charlotte potatoes
- Fine sea salt to taste
- Freshly ground white pepper to taste
- Freshly grated nutmeg to taste
- 4 tablespoons peanut oil

TO FINISH

- 1/2 pound (250 g) smoked salmon,
  cut into 12 thin slices
- 4 tablespoons whipped cream
- 2 ounces (60 g) Oscietra caviar
- 12 leaves flat-leaf parsley, washed

SPECIAL MATERIAL

- 4 nonstick blini pans, each 5 inches
  (12 1/2 cm) in diameter

Wine suggestion: a rosé Champagne.

Egg Cups of Lobster with Quail Eggs and Caviar

BY CHRISTOPHE CUSSAC

Cook the lobster: in a large pot, bring the court bouillon to a rolling boil. Remove the bands restraining the lobster claws and plunge the lobster, head first, into the liquid. Cook for 1 minute. Remove the pot from heat, and leave the lobster to stand in the court bouillon for 30 minutes to 1 hour.

Drain the lobster. Twist off each claw. Crack the claw shells with a nutcracker. Extract the meat with a seafood fork – it should come out in a single piece. Detach the tail from the rest of the body. With scissors, carefully cut lengthwise down the tail to extract the tail meat in one piece. With a small knife, remove the intestinal tract from the lower area of the tail meat.

Dice the lobster meat. In a small bowl, blend the mayonnaise and ketchup. Add the lobster meat and mix to blend. Taste for seasoning. Fill each egg cup halfway with the lobster mixture. Cover with plastic wrap and refrigerate.

Prepare the toasts: preheat the broiler. Broil the brioche "batonnets" until golden. Set aside.

Prepare the sauce: in a medium-size saucepan, combine the wine and vermouth. Add the shallot and reduce the liquid by half over medium heat. Add the mussel juices and the cream.

Lower the heat and reduce the mixture until it thickens slightly. Taste for seasoning. Strain into a small saucepan. Set aside and keep warm.

Heat the egg cups: preheat the oven on the lowest setting possible. Place the egg cups in center of the oven and heat for 5 minutes.

Cook the quail eggs: in a non-stick pan, heat the butter and carefully add the cracked quails eggs. Cover and cook gently over low heat for 1 minute.

Remove the egg cups from the oven. Add one third of the caviar and the salmon eggs to the egg cups. Return to the oven and heat for a maximum of 1 minute, taking care that the caviar warms but does not cook.

Blend the remaining two-thirds of caviar into the sauce and reheat without boiling.

Trim the edges of the eggs with scissors so they fit perfectly into each egg cup. Place an egg on top of each egg cup. Spoon the sauce around each yolk. Serve immediately with the toasted brioche.

4 SERVINGS

FOR THE LOBSTER

- One 1-pound (500 g) lobster, rinsed
- 1 quart (1 l) court bouillon
- 1 tablespoon mayonnaise
- 1 tablespoon ketchup

FOR THE TOASTS

- 4 slices of brioche, cut into
  16 "batonnets"

FOR THE SAUCE

- 4 tablespoons white wine
- 4 tablespoons vermouth (Noilly Prat)
- 1 small shallot, peeled and minced
- 4 tablespoons cooking juices from mussels
- 1 tablespoon heavy cream

FOR THE EGGS

- 2 tablespoons (30 g) unsalted butter
- 12 fresh quail eggs

TO FINISH

- 3 tablespoons caviar
- 1 tablespoon salmon eggs
- Fine sea salt
- Freshly ground pepper

SPECIAL MATERIAL

- 12 egg cups

Wine suggestion: a white Burgundy, a grand cru Chablis.

Spider Crab with Caviar

BY PHILIPPE GROULT

Prepare the court bouillon: in a large stockpot, bring the water to a rolling boil over high heat. Add the carrot, onion, lime zest, lemon zest, ginger root, thyme, bay leaves and black peppercorns. Cook for 3 minutes. Add the white wine and the vinegar and bring to a boil over high heat. Reduce and simmer gently for 10 minutes.

Cook the crabs: Bring the court bouillon to a rolling boil over high heat. Rinse the four 1-pound male crabs under cold running water. Plunge the crabs, head first, into the court bouillon.
Counting from the time the crabs hit the water, cook for 12 minutes. With a large flat-mesh skimmer, remove the crabs and drain. With a ladle, skim off any impurities that rise to the surface. Repeat the same procedure for the female crabs, and then for the larger male crabs. Set aside.

Prepare a large bowl of ice water. Bring the court bouillon to a rolling boil over high heat, add the seaweed and cook for 30 seconds, or until it changes color. Remove with a slotted spoon, and plunge it into the ice water to cool. As soon as the seaweed is cool, drain and set it aside.

Shell the crabs: prepare 2 medium-sized bowls. Begin with smaller male crabs. The shells of the 1 pound males will be used for presentation, so it is not necessary to remove the meat from inside the claws. Simply cut around the edge of each head and remove the top part of the shell. Keep back the liquid and any coral found in the heads. Reserve the liquid in a bowl. Set aside. Pull away the shell on the undersection of each crab, remove the flesh and place in another bowl. Set aside.

Prepare the crabs for presentation. Set each crab upright on a flat work surface and cut around the edges where the head was using scissors. Rinse the shells under cold running water and set aside.

Shell the remaining crabs: with a spoon, remove the eggs from the undersides of the female crabs. Set aside. For the remaining 8 crabs, gently crack the claws with a nutcracker or hammer, trying not to damage the meat. Extract the meat with a seafood fork, taking care to remove any shell fragments. All of the crabmeat may be collected in the same bowl. The creamy liquid and the coral from the head area should be put in a separate bowl. When all of the crabs have been shelled, discard the remaining 8 shells.

Prepare the crab cream: in a large bowl, whisk together the head liquid, the coral and half the eggs until the texture is relatively smooth. Add 5 tablespoons olive oil in a thin stream, whisking until well blended. Whisk in the lemon juice. Season with salt and pepper to taste. Transfer the mixture to a large bowl. Set aside.

Pick through the crabmeat one last time, making sure there are no tough bits or shell fragments. With a whisk, incorporate half of the crabmeat into the crab cream. Taste for seasoning. Set aside. Prepare the garnish: place the caviar in a small bowl. Add the remaining olive oil half the chives and mix to blend. Set aside. To serve: arrange a small bed of seaweed on 4 large dinner plates. Place an empty crab shell in the center of each plate. Spoon the crab cream into the head cavity and place the remaining crabmeat on top. Spoon the caviar over the cream.

Sprinkle with the remaining chives. Serve immediately.

4 SERVINGS

THE COURT-BOUILLON

- 7 quarts (7 l) water
- 1 carrot, peeled and chopped
- 1 onion, peeled and chopped
- Zest of half a lime
- Zest of half a lemon
- 1/2 teaspoon grated fresh ginger root
- 1 small bunch fresh thyme, washed
- 2 bay leaves
- 1 teaspoon whole black peppercorns
- 1 quart (1 l) dry white wine
- 2 cups (50 cl) white vinegar

THE CRABS

- 4 male spider crabs, each weighing 1 pound (500 g), scrubbed and washed
- 4 female spider crabs with eggs, each weighing 2 pounds (1 kg), scrubbed and washed
- 4 male spider crabs, each weighing 2 pounds (1 kg), scrubbed and washed
- 10 ounces (300 g) fresh seaweed, thoroughly washed

THE CRAB CREAM

- 6 tablespoons (9.5 cl) extra-virgin olive oil
- Juice of 1 lemon, strained

THE GARNISH

- 7 ounces (200g) caviar
- 1 tablespoon minced chives
- Fine sea salt
- Freshly ground pepper

Wine suggestion: a rosé Champagne.

Apple, Caviar, and Red Onion Salad

BY BENOÎT GUICHARD

With a sharp knife or a mandoline, cut the onions crosswise into paper-thin slices. Separate into rings.

Place the onions in a small sieve and sprinkle with fine salt. Set aside to drain for 15 minutes. Rinse the onions under cold water and drain. Transfer to a small bowl, add 2 tablespoons of lemon juice and 6 tablespoons (1 dl) of oil and toss to blend. Set aside. (The onions can be prepared 2 to 3 days in advance, covered and refrigerated.)

Prepare a vinaigrette: in a small bowl, whisk together 2 tablespoons lemon juice and a pinch of salt. Slowly blend in the heavy cream. Whisk 4 tablespoons of oil in a thin stream, whisking until emulsified. The vinaigrette should be quite acidic. Set aside.

Peel, core, and halve the apples lengthwise. With a mandoline, cut into paper-thin, half-moon slices. Transfer to a small bowl, toss with the remaining 2 tablespoons lemon juice. Season lightly with salt and pepper. Set aside.

Place a 3-inch (7 1/2 cm) round pastry cutter (to use as a template) in the center of a dinner plate. Arrange 14 overlapping apple slices within the pastry cutter, working in a circular pattern. Repeat for the remaining 3 servings.

With a small spoon, top the apple slices with an even layer of caviar.

In a medium-size bowl, combine the purslane and arugula. Add just enough vinaigrette to coat the greens. Toss to coat evenly.

Drizzle each plate with vinaigrette. Top the caviar with several onion rings and dill fronds. Arrange a bundle of greens on top of the onion rings. Serve immediately.

4 SERVINGS

- 3 small red onions, peeled
- Sea salt to taste
- 6 tablespoons (1 dl) freshly squeezed lemon juice
- 10 tablespoons (16 cl) extra-virgin olive oil
- 2 tablespoons heavy cream
- Freshly ground white pepper to taste
- 2 Granny Smith apples
- 1 1/2 ounces (45 g) Oscietra caviar
- A handful of arugula (about 1 ounce; 30 g)
- A handful of purslane (about 1 ounce; 30 g)
- 16 dill fronds

SPECIAL MATERIAL:

- One 3-inch (7 1/2 cm) round pastry cutter, to use as a template

Wine suggestion: a fine, vintage Champagne, blanc de blanc.

Cannelloni of Sea Trout with Caviar

BY MAURICE GUILLOUËT

Prepare the sea trout: cut 4 rectangles, about 4 inches (10 cm) by 5 inches (12 1/2 cm). Each portion should weigh between 3 to 4 ounces (100 to 125 g). Spread 1/2 ounce (15 g) caviar on each, season with pepper and roll each "cannelloni" in plastic wrap lightly coated with olive oil. Refrigerate.

Prepare the sauce: in a saucepan, heat 1 tablespoon unsalted butter over moderate heat. Add the onion and fennel and cook gently, 3 to 5 minutes, without browning. Season lightly. Cover and cook an additional 10 minutes, stirring from time to time. Add the fish stock and the cream and simmer, uncovered, for 15 minutes. Pass through a fine mesh seive into another skillet and reduce slightly. Taste for seasoning. Remove the saucepan from the heat, and whisk in the tablespoon of cold butter.

Return the butter to low heat whisking until the butter has melted. Keep warm.

Bring 1 quart (1 l) of water to a simmer in the bottom of a steamer. Carefully arrange the cannelloni in a single layer in the top of the steamer. Place the top over simmering water, cover, and steam until the cannelloni are just warmed through, about 4 minutes. They should be slightly underdone. Drain and trim neatly. Cut on a diagonal to make neat edges. Remove and discard the plastic wrap.

To serve: place each cannelloni on a warmed dinner plate. Spoon the sauce around them. Sprinkle each plate with remaining caviar and the fresh dill. Serve immediately.

4 SERVINGS

- 22 sea trout fillets, each 10 to 12 ounces (300-360 g)
- 2 ounces (60 g) caviar
- 1 teaspoon extra-virgin olive oil

THE SAUCE
- 1 tablespoon (1/2 ounce; 15 g) unsalted butter
- 1 small onion, peeled and minced
- 1 small fennel bulb, washed, halved and minced
- 1 cup (25 cl) fish stock
- 1 cup (25 cl) heavy cream
- 1 tablespoon (1/2 ounce; 15 g) unsalted butter, chilled
- Coarse sea salt
- Freshly ground pepper

TO FINISH
- 2 sprigs fresh dill
- 1 1/2 ounces (25 g) caviar

Wine suggestion: a white Burgundy, such as a rich and fruity Pouilly Fuisse.

Scallops roasted in their Shells with Herbs and Butter

BY JOËL ROBUCHON

4 SERVINGS

INGREDIENTS

- **12 fresh scallops in their shell, without coral**
- **12 tablespoons (6 ounces; 180 g) unsalted butter, softened**
- **Sea salt and freshly ground white pepper to taste**
- **1/2 carrot, peeled and cut into a fine julienne**
- **4 spring onions, peeled**
- **1/4 cucumber, peeled and cut into a fine julienne**
- **Zest (grated peel) of half a lime**
- **1 ounce (30 g) dried vermicelli**
- **6 tablespoons (1 dl) orange juice**
- **3 tablespoons dry white wine**
- **1 tablespoon anise liqueur (Pastis)**
- **4 tablespoons (2 ounces; 60 g) unsalted butter, clarified**
- **1 bunch of seaweed (optional)**

To open the scallops: place a small knife on an angle so it hugs the interior of the flat, top shell. With one deft motion, slide the knife down the wall of the shell, detaching the scallop on one side. Remove and discard the top shell. With a tablespoon, remove the "beard" and the little muscle on the side but leave the scallop attached to the bottom of its shell. Rinse the "beards" and the scallops separately under cold water. Drain.

To make the scallops easier to eat and to keep them in place, partially detach them from their shells: with a small knife, detach 3/4 of the scallop muscle from the shell. Place a bit of softened butter on the underside of the scallop still partially attached to the shell. Season the underside with salt and pepper. With a brush, coat the top of each scallop liberally with the softened butter. Season with salt and pepper. Refrigerate.

Prepare a large bowl of ice water. Bring a large pot of water to a boil. Salt, and add the carrot. Blanch until tender, about 1 minute. Remove with a slotted spoon and place in the ice water just long enough to cool down. Drain, and set aside. Repeat, blanching the onions, cucumbers and lime zest separately in new batches of boiling, salted water. Drain, and set aside.

Bring a large pot of water to a rolling boil. Salt, and add the vermicelli. Cook until tender but firm to the bite, or al dente. Drain and set aside.

In a small saucepan, combine the orange juice, wine, Pastis and the scallop "beards." Cover, bring to a simmer over moderate heat and poach for 1 minute. Remove from the heat, cover and set aside to infuse 15 minutes. Drain the "beards;" dice finely. Set aside. Separately, reserve the poaching liquid.

In a large skillet, heat the clarified butter over moderately high heat, just until it bubbles lightly. Add the drained pasta and cook, tossing frequently, until very lightly and evenly browned and crispy, 5 to 8 minutes. Drain and set aside.

Bring a large pot of water to a rolling boil. Add the seaweed and blanch for 30 seconds. Refresh in cold water. Drain and set aside.

Preheat the oven to 425°F (220°C; gas mark 7/8).

Place 12 round cookie cutters or other small, round, ovenproof objects (to serve as stands to stabilize the scallops as they roast) on a baking sheet. Place a scallop shell in each stand. Season each scallop with a sprinkling of thyme leaves. Place in the center of the oven and roast just long enough to firm them up without cooking them fully, about 45 seconds.

Remove the baking sheet from the oven and carefully pour any cooking juices from each scallop into the reserved poaching liquid. Return each scallop to its stand on the baking sheet.

Seasoning

- 1/2 teaspoon fresh thyme leaves
- 1 tablespoon fresh ginger root, cut into a fine julienne
- 2 tablespoons finely chopped fresh dill
- About 12 tablespoons coarse sea salt
- Fleur de sel de Guérande
- Coarsely ground white pepper

● Using a well sharpened knife, cut the vegetables into a fine julienne.

● Set the julienne of vegetables and the vermicelli apart.

● Slide the blade of a small sharp knife into the edge of the scallop shell.

● Remove the "beard," leaving the scallop attached to the bottom of its shell.

● Remove the little muscle located on the side of each scallop and discard it.

● Holding the shell, partially detach the scallop muscle from the bottom of the shell.

● Using a brush, coat the top of each scallop with the softened butter and season.

● Cook the vermicelli in boiling water until tender but firm to the bite.

Add the chopped scallop "beards" to the poaching liquid, along with the julienne of vegetables, lime zest, ginger, and half of the minced dill. Add another drop of Pastis to perk up the flavor. Taste for seasoning.

To prepare the plates: in a small bowl, combine the coarse sea salt with enough water to allow the grains to adhere to one another. Spoon the moistened salt into three small mounds on each plate. (This will help the shells stay in place as the scallops are eaten.)

Arrange a few leaves of seaweed in the center of each plate, slightly overlapping the salt mounds.

● In a small saucepan, combine the orange juice with the white wine and the Pastis.

● Add the "beards" and let them infuse in this mixture.

● Carefully drain the "beards" with a skimmer before chopping them finely.

● Saute the vermicelli until it becomes lightly browned and crispy.

Just before serving, return the scallops to the oven and roast for 1 to 2 minutes for slightly underdone scallops; 3 to 4 minutes for fully cooked scallops. Place each shell on the salt mounds on the prepared plates. Spoon the sauce around the edge of each scallop.

Garnish each edge with the vegetable mixture, then sprinkle with the crispy vermicelli. Carefully season each scallop with fleur de sel, coarsely ground white pepper and the remaining dill. Serve immediately.

SEAWEED

For decoration, a few leaves of blanched seaweed are placed in the center of each plate, slightly overlapping the salt mounds.

Wine suggestion: a fine white Burgundy, such as an elegant, full-bodied, Meursault 1er Cru.

● Blanch the seaweed for 30 seconds in boiling water.

● Place the scallop shells on cookie cutters to stabilize them during the cooking.

● Add the cooking juices from the scallops to the reserved poaching liquid with the "beards."

● Garnish each scallop with the sauce, the vegetable mixture and the crisp vermicelli.

❝ THE SCALLOP PERFECTLY REFLECTS THE CUISINE OF JOEL ROBUCHON: AT ONCE SIMPLE, MYSTERIOUS, PURE AND HARMONIOUS, THE SCALLOP FREELY DISPERSES ITS GUSTATIVE QUALITIES, DISTINGUISHED BY THEIR RICHNESS AND INTENSITY. ❞

SUMMARY

● Joël Robuchon ●

With his Noix de Saint-Jacques cuites en coquilles aux aromates, Joël Robuchon displays his penchant for foods that are pure and simple, allowing the main ingredient to speak for itself. The scallops are oven-baked in their shells — whole, like a fish cooked in its entirety or a chicken cooked on the bone. The naturally sweet flavor of the scallop comes through, balanced by a sweet-and-sour sauce of orange and lime juice, white wine, a touch of ginger and anise, all tempered by julienned vegetables.

● Dominique Bouchet ●

Dominque Bouchet, with his "Quenelles de Saint-Jacques sur purée de champignons," returns to a theme from to the early days of Jamin, one that the master later abandoned. While Joël Robuchon's creation maintains a strong connection with the scallop in its raw state, by serving it in its shell, Dominique Bouchet creates a scallop puree poached in the form of quenelles. He places the quenelles on a bed of mushroom puree, bringing out the earthy, "sea-air" taste of the scallops and maintaining a connection with the raw ingredient.

• Christophe Cussac •

With his "Noix de Saint-Jacques aux citrons confits et chips de pomme de terre," Christophe Cussac retains a valuable lesson from his master: the importance of texture and the pleasure of contrasts united on a single plate. He surrounds his scallops with thin potato chips, a sprinkling of bacon and the zest of lemon confit, adding a salty, crispy element to the dish. With the addition of the delicious lemon confit – borrowed from Moroccan cuisine and treated in a French manner – Christophe Cussac displays a tendency to be influenced by international elements.

• Benoît Guichard •

Benoît Guichard, with his "Noix de Saint-Jacques grillées, salade de jeunes fenouils tiède," picks up the theme of Joël Robuchon's "invisible cuisine," food that looks easy but is far from being so. The scallops are meticulously grilled and seasoned, then sautéed to enhance the earthy quality of the mushroom. The dish is carefully constructed, every step calculated so that each ingredient gives the best of its own authentic flavor. The scallops are served on a bed of fennel puree with a tangy and very modern blend of julienned vegetables: horseradish, radish and fennel.

• Philippe Groult •

Philippe Groult tangles with the same question of acidity and sweetness in his "Noix de Saint-Jacques et anguille fumée en brochette." The scallops are grilled, giving them a smoky taste and bringing them closer to their accompaniment: smoked eel. The other elements are important: a small salad of arugula and watercress provides a tangy, acidic touch. The two sauces – a reduction of balsamic vinegar and a separate reduction of melon and port – counterbalance the fish with sweetness and strong flavor.

• Maurice Guillouët •

If one were to imagine Robuchon's creation without the shells, it would be Maurice Guillouët's "Ravioli de Saint-Jacques au beurre de légumes." The scallops are enveloped instead, in a protective layer of pasta, to seal in the flavor as they cook. The sauce juxtaposes the sweetness of butter, carrots, and shallots against the acidity of bell pepper, as Robuchon does with anise and orange juice.

Scallop Quenelles on a Bed of Mushroom Puree

BY DOMINIQUE BOUCHET

Prepare the scallops: rinse the scallops and pat dry. Remove and discard the little muscle on the side.

Place the scallops in a food processor. Season with salt and pepper. Blend to obtain a smooth mixture, 3 to 4 minutes, pulsing on and off. Add the egg whites and mix again to blend. Add the heavy cream and double cream and mix to blend. Transfer to a small bowl. Refrigerate.

Prepare the mushroom puree: in a large skillet, melt the butter over moderate heat. Sweat the shallot. Add the mushrooms and stir with a wooden spoon. Cook over high heat, stirring constantly, 2 minutes. Add the lemon juice. Season to taste. Reduce heat and cook until the excess liquid has evaporated.

Cook the scallops: in a large stockpot, heat the fish stock over a medium heat. When the stock reaches a gentle simmer, use a tablespoon to shape eight quenelles of the scallop mixture. Drop the quenelles into the warmed fish stock and cook, uncovered, for 5 minutes.

Prepare the sabayon: in a saucepan, reduce the Sauternes over high heat until 4 tablespoons remain. Whisk in the egg yolk and cook, whisking constantly until the mixture forms a mousse. With a spatula, gently fold in the whipped cream. Taste for seasoning. Set aside.

Divide the mushroom puree evenly among four individual gratin dishes. Even out with the back of a spoon. Place two quenelles on top of the mushroom mixture. Evenly divide the sabayon, pouring it uniformly over the quenelles. Place under the broiler and brown lightly. Serve immediately.

4 SERVINGS

THE SCALLOPS

- 7 ounces (200 g) scallops

- 1/2 teaspoon fine sea salt

- Freshly ground pepper

- 2 egg whites

- 4 tablespoons heavy cream

- 3 tablespoons double cream

- 6 cups (1.5 liters) fish stock

THE MUSHROOM PUREE

- 1 tablespoon (15 g) unsalted butter

- 1 small shallot, peeled and minced

- 3/4 pound (375 g) mushrooms

- Cultivated mushrooms, peeled, washed and finely chopped

- 1 teaspoon freshly squeezed lemon juice

THE SABAYON

- 1 cup (25 cl) Sauternes wine

- 1 egg yolk

- 4 tablespoons cream, whipped

SPECIAL MATERIAL

- 4 small gratin dishes

Wine suggestion: a white from the Rhône valley, such as a Saint-Joseph.

Scallops with Lemon Confit and Potato Chips

BY CHRISTOPHE CUSSAC

In a small bowl, toss together sugar and salt. Roll the lemon quarters in the mixture. Cover and store in a cool, dry place for 3 weeks, tossing from time to time.

Prepare the potato chips: peel and thinly slice the potato. Rinse and pat dry. Season with salt and pepper. In a large skillet, heat half the clarified butter until it sizzles. Add the potatoes and fry over moderate heat until golden brown, tossing often. Drain. Set aside.

Prepare the garnish: in a medium-size skillet, heat the remaining clarified butter over moderate heat. Add the leek and fry, tossing constantly, until crispy, 6 to 8 minutes. Drain. Set aside.

Trim the zest from the cured lemons and cut into a fine julienne. Set aside.

Fill a small saucepan with water and bring to a boil over high heat. Add the bacon and blanch for 30 seconds. Drain. Heat a small skillet until hot but not smoking. Add the bacon and cook until golden brown, 3 to 5 minutes. Drain. Set aside.

Prepare the sauce: in a non-stick pan, heat the oil over high heat, add the scallop beards and sauté, tossing constantly until evenly browned, 2 to 3 minutes. Add the shallot and cook, covered, for

an additional 5 minutes. Add the white wine and cook, uncovered for 3 minutes. Add the chicken stock and the bouquet garni and cook for 20 minutes. Pass the mixture through a fine mesh sieve into a small saucepan and reduce until the liquid equals 4 tablespoons. Set aside.

In a large non-stick skillet, heat 4 tablespoons (50 g) butter over medium heat until it sizzles. Season the scallops and sear over moderately high heat, basting them frequently as they cook. Drain and keep warm. Add the cooking juices to the reduced sauce.

Prepare the garnish: in a large pot, bring 6 quarts of water to a rolling boil. Add salt and blanch the spinach for 30 seconds. Shock in ice water, then drain the spinach and press into balls to rid of excess moisture. Set aside. Heat a large skillet until hot but not smoking. Add 4 tablespoons (50 g) butter and cook until it turns brown ("noisette"). If the casserole is hot, this should happen almost instantly. Add the spinach and mix briskly for one minute with a fork pierced with a whole garlic clove.

To serve: arrange the spinach in the center of each of the four warmed dinner plates. Arrange the scallops on top of the spinach. Arrange the potato chips vertically around the center. Sprinkle with the bacon and lemon peel. Spoon the sauce alongside. Serve immediately.

4 SERVINGS

LEMON CONFIT

- 2 teaspoons sugar
- 1/2 cup (100 g) fine sea salt
- 4 lemons, washed and quartered lengthwise

THE POTATO CHIPS

- One large 10-ounce (300 g) Bintje potato
- Sea salt and freshly ground white pepper to taste
- 8 tablespoons (120 g) clarified butter

THE SCALLOPS

- 1 pound (500 g) scallops, rinsed, drained and beards reserved
- 7 tablespoons (100 g) unsalted butter

THE SAUCE

- 2 tablespoons extra-virgin olive oil
- The reserved scallop beards, rinsed and drained
- 1 shallot, peeled and minced
- 6 tablespoons (1 dl) white wine
- 1 cup (25 cl) chicken stock
- Bouquet garni

THE GARNISH

- 1 leek, cleaned and cut into a very fine julienne
- 1 1/2 pounds (750 g) fresh spinach, washed, with large ribs removed
- 1 garlic clove, peeled and stuck on the end of a fork
- 3 ounces (90 g) slab bacon, rind removed

Wine suggestion: a wine from the Loire valley, such as a well-balanced white Sancerre.

Skewers of Scallops and Smoked Eel

BY PHILIPPE GROULT

Carefully rinse the scallops and pat dry. Remove and discard the little muscle on the side of the scallops. Set aside. Rinse the coral and beards thoroughly under cold running water. Set aside.

In a medium-size saucepan, heat the olive oil until hot, but not smoking. Add the onion and cook over moderate heat until softened, 5 minutes. Add the beards, coral, instant chicken stock, fennel seeds and star anise and cook 3 minutes more. With a wooden spoon, mix to blend. Season lightly. Add 5 cups of water and simmer, uncovered, 20 minutes.

Remove the pan from the heat and set aside for 10 minutes to allow impurities to settle to the bottom. Line a sieve with a moistened cheesecloth, set the sieve over a large bowl and strain. Return the strained stock to the pan. Simmer over moderate heat until reduced by 3/4, about 25 minutes. Set aside.

Prepare the sauces: in a medium-size saucepan, add the balsamic vinegar and reduce over moderate heat until syrupy and thick in consistency. Set aside. In another saucepan, combine the melon juice and the port over moderate heat. Reduce by half. Set aside. In a small skillet, heat the butter over moderate heat until melted. Add the breadcrumbs and cook until golden brown on both sides, 3 to 5 minutes, turning once. Add the Szechuan peppercorns and toss to coat thoroughly. Remove and transfer to paper towels to drain. Set aside.

Fry the sage leaves: pour the peanut oil into a large, heavy-bottomed saucepan. Place a deep-fry thermometer in the oil and heat to 320° F (160° C). Fry the sage leaves in small batches, 1 to 2 minutes. With a wire skimmer, lift the leaves from the oil and drain. Season with sea salt. Set aside. Heat a large, non-stick skillet over moderate heat. Add the olive oil.

Season the scallops with salt and pepper and sear them over medium heat, browning them on both sides, about 2 to 3 minutes on each side. Add the bacon slices, tossing lightly to blend. Remove and drain.

Preparing the skewers: note that one end of the scallop is wider than the other. Carefully place 1 scallop on each of the 4 skewers. Follow with a piece of smoked eel, a leaf of fried sage and another scallop on each skewer. Continue to alternate the scallops, eel and sage on each skewer until all ingredients have been used, taking care that the scallops are arranged uniformly. Press the skewered items tightly together, so they are securely attached and do not turn easily. Sprinkle with the breadcrumbs.

Preheat the oven to the lowest setting possible, about 210° F (100° C; gas mark 1). Lay the skewers in an ovenproof pan and put them in the oven with the door ajar.

Prepare the salad: in a small bowl, combine the arugula and watercress. Pour the vinaigrette over the salad and toss thoroughly until all the greens are lightly but evenly coated. Cut each slice of bacon into several even pieces.

To serve: mound the greens on warmed dinner plates and top with the bacon and onion slices. Spoon a few drops of the reduced balsamic vinegar on top. Spoon the reduced melon juice and the reduced scallop stock side-by-side on the plates around the salad. Place a skewer on top of the sauces. Serve immediately.

4 SERVINGS

THE SCALLOPS

- 20 large fresh scallops (1 1/2 to 2 inches),
  shelled, coral and beard reserved

THE SCALLOPS STOCK

- 6 tablespoons (4 cl) extra-virgin olive oil
- 1 onion, peeled and chopped
- 1 cube instant chicken stock
- 1/4 teaspoon fennel seeds
- 1 star anise

THE SAUCES

- 1 quart (1 l) balsamic vinegar
- 1 melon, peeled, seeded and juiced
- 1 2/3 cups (41 cl) port
- 3 tablespoons (1 1/2 ounces; 45 g)
  unsalted butter
- 1 1/2 ounces (45 g) homemade breadcrumbs
- 1/2 teaspoon Szechuan peppercorns

THE SKEWERS

- 1 1/4 cups (31 cl) peanut oil, for frying
- 20 leaves fresh sage, washed and
  thoroughly dried
- 4 thin slices bacon, grilled until crispy
- 1 fillet smoked eel, cut into 12 small pieces

THE SALAD

- 3 ounces (90 g) fresh arugula, trimmed
  and washed
- 1 small bunch watercress, trimmed and washed
- 2 tablespoons vinaigrette
- 1 baby onion, peeled and cut into thin rounds

*Wine suggestion: a seductive white from Alsace,
a Gewurztraminer.*

Grilled Scallops with warm Fennel salad

BY BENOÎT GUICHARD

Prepare the onion relish: slice the onion in half lengthwise. Place each half, cut side down, on a cutting board and cut crosswise into very thin slices. Place the onion in a small strainer and season generously with fine sea salt. Place the strainer in a bowl and set aside for 1 hour to drain. Rinse and drain the onions. Place in a small bowl and toss with the lemon juice. Set aside and refrigerate.

Prepare the fennel puree: in a large pot, bring 6 quarts of water to a boil. Add 3 tablespoons sea salt and the coarsely chopped fennel. Cook until very soft, about 10 minutes. Drain. Puree in a food mill or food processor. Set aside.

Prepare the fennel for the salad: cut the fennel into a fine julienne. Bring 3 quarts (3 l) of water to a boil. Add 1 1/2 tablespoons sea salt and blanch the fennel for about 30 seconds. Transfer to a large colander and refresh under cold running water. Drain. Set aside. Carefully rinse the scallops. Note that one end of the scallop is wider than the other. Carefully place 4 scallops on each of 4 skewers, taking care to arrange the scallops uniformly, with the widest ends always side-by-side. Press them tightly together, so they are securely attached to the skewers and do not turn easily. Place on a clean plate, cover and refrigerate.

Prepare the horseradish vinaigrette: in a small bowl, combine the vinegar, horseradish, oil and a pinch of salt. Whisk to blend. Season with a few drops of Worcestershire sauce. Taste for seasoning. Set aside. At serving time, transfer the fennel puree to a small saucepan. Whisk in the cream. Warm gently over very low heat and whisk in just enough vinaigrette to add a pleasant acidity. (You will

probably not need all the vinaigrette.) Taste for seasoning. Add the reserved chopped fennel fronds and stir to blend.

Cover and set aside to keep warm, or keep warm in a bain marie.

In a small saucepan, combine half the chopped fennel fronds, the blanched fennel, the black radish, and the horseradish vinaigrette. Drain the red onion relish and add to the other vegetables. Toss to blend and warm gently over low heat.

Preheat the top grill of a gas, electric, or ridged, cast-iron stove. Or, prepare a wood or charcoal fire. The fire is ready when the coals glow red and are covered with ash.

Season the scallops with salt, pepper, thyme and drizzle them with olive oil. Place each skewer on the grill at a 45° angle to the ridges of the grill. Grill for 1 minute. Still grilling the same side of the scallops, reposition each skewer to the alternate 45° angle. Grill for 1 minute more. (This will form a very even and attractive grill mark on each side of the scallop.) Transfer the skewers to a clean plate. Turn them over and grill on the other side, positioning the scallops again at the two angles, grilling for a total of 2 minutes more.

To serve, place a mound of dressed julienned vegetables on the top of each of the 4 warmed dinner plates. Place a dollop of fennel puree on the bottom of the plate. Carefully remove the scallops from the skewers and set on top of the puree. Season each scallop with a bit of coarsely ground black pepper, a few grains of fleur de sel and several drops of lemon juice. Serve immediately.

4 SERVINGS

ONION RELISH

- 1 red onion, peeled
- Sea salt to taste
- 2 tablespoons freshly squeezed lemon juice

FENNEL PUREE

- 1 large bulb fennel, fronds reserved
- 3 tablespoons sea salt
- 1/4 cup (6 cl) heavy cream

SALAD

- 8 miniature fennel bulbs or 4 small fennel bulbs, fronds reserved
- 1 1/2 tablespoons sea salt
- 1/2 black radish, peeled and julienned
- 16 fresh scallops, without coral, shelled

HORSERADISH VINAIGRETTE

- 1/4 cup (6 cl) best quality sherry wine vinegar
- 1 tablespoon prepared horseradish
- 1/4 cup (6 cl) extra-virgin olive oil
- Fine sea salt to taste
- Several drops Worcestershire sauce

CLASSIC VINAIGRETTE

- 1 tablespoon sherry wine vinegar
- 3 tablespoons extra virgin olive oil
- Fine sea salt to taste

FINAL SEASONING

- Salt and freshly ground white pepper to taste
- 1/4 teaspoon fresh thyme leaves
- Extra-virgin olive oil
- Coarsely ground black pepper
- Fleur de sel
- Freshly squeezed lemon juice

Wine suggestion: a dry white Cassis from Provence.

Scallop Ravioli with Vegetable Butter

BY MAURICE GUILLOUËT

Preheat oven to 200° F (80° C; gas mark 1). Arrange tomato quarters on baking sheet. Season with salt, pepper, and confectioners' sugar. Scatter with thyme and place a garlic sliver on each quarter. Drizzle with oil.

Place in the oven and cook until very soft, about 1 hour. Turn, baste, and cook until tender, about 2 hours total. They should remain moist and soft. Remove from the oven to cool. Remove skin and mince. Set aside.

Sift flour onto work surface and make a well: add goose fat, hot water and salt to the well. With a fork, mix to form a soft dough. Transfer to a lightly floured surface and knead until satiny and resilient, 10 to 15 minutes. Cover and set aside for 1 hour.

In a skillet, heat 3 tablespoons of the butter over a moderate heat. Add the shallots, carrots, celery and leeks and cook, covered, for 10 minutes, mixing from time to time. Taste for seasoning. Remove from the heat. Set aside.

Blanch the red pepper in salted boiling water for 2 minutes. Refresh. Repeat with green pepper. Set aside.

Season scallops with salt, pepper, and thyme. Cover each with a parsley leaf. Set aside. Place dough on a work surface. Roll very fine. Arrange scallops on pasta. Cover with another layer of pasta. Cut with a 3-inch (7 1/2 cm) round cookie cutter. Pinch with your fingers to assure a firm closure. Place on lightly floured pan. Refrigerate.

Heat diced tomato in a skillet over moderate heat, add the tomato confit and cook, 2 minutes. Taste for seasoning.

Place skillet with diced vegetables over moderate heat. Incorporate the remaining 6 tablespoons butter. Add peppers, reserving some for presentation. Season with salt and pepper.

In a large pot, bring 6 quarts (6 l) of water to a rolling boil. Add 3 tablespoons salt and the ravioli, stirring gently to prevent the ravioli from sticking together. Cook for 3 minutes. Drain.

To serve: n each warmed dinner plate, dress five ravioli in a circle. Spoon the vegetable butter over them and finish with the tomato garnish. Sprinkle with the reserved diced peppers. Serve immediately.

4 SERVINGS

TOMATO CONFIT

- 6 oval tomatoes, cored, seeded and quartered
- Sea salt
- Freshly ground pepper
- A pinch of confectioners' sugar
- 2 sprigs fresh thyme, stemmed
- 2 fresh, plump garlic cloves, peeled and slivered
- 2 tablespoons extra-virgin olive oil

RAVIOLI

- 2 cups (265 g) unbleached all-purpose flour
- 1/2 ounce (15 g) goose fat
- 6 tablespoons (9.5 cl) hot water
- 1/4 teaspoon fine sea salt

- 9 tablespoons (4 1/2 ounces; 135 g) unsalted butter
- 2 shallots, peeled, diced
- 2 carrots, washed, peeled, diced
- 2 sticks celery, washed, diced
- 2 leeks, the white and tender green parts, washed, diced
- 1 small red bell pepper, washed, trimmed, diced
- 1 small green bell pepper, washed, trimmed, diced
- 20 large fresh sea scallops, rinsed, patted dry, small muscle removed
- 20 leaves fresh flat-leaf parsley, stemmed and washed
- 1/2 teaspoon fresh thyme, stemmed
- Diced tomato

SPECIAL MATERIAL

- 1 round cutter, 3 inches (7.5 cm) in diameter

Wine suggestion: a grand and delicate white from the Loire valley, such as a Bonnezeaux.

Grilled Wild Mushrooms with Thyme and Eggplant Caviar

BY JOËL ROBUCHON

4 SERVINGS

INGREDIENTS

- 1 1/4 pounds (750 g) fresh, firm eggplant, washed but not peeled
- 5 plump, fresh garlic cloves, peeled and slivered
- 1/4 cup (6 cl) extra-virgin olive oil
- 1 plump, fresh garlic clove, peeled and minced
- 1 teaspoon fresh thyme leaves
- Sea salt and freshly ground white pepper to taste
- A pinch of curry powder
- 1 tablespoon mayonnaise
- 4 baby eggplants, washed but not peeled
- 1 1/4 cups (31 cl) peanut oil for frying
- 1 tablespoon flour
- 2 pounds (1 kg) portobello (cèpe) mushrooms, rinsed and peeled
- 4 tablespoons (2 ounces; 60 g) unsalted butter
- Fleur de sel

Preheat the oven to 400° F (200° C; gas mark 6/7).

With a small knife, make incisions at regular intervals in the eggplant, and fill each incision with a garlic half.

Place the eggplant directly on the baking rack and bake the eggplant until very soft, turning the eggplant from time to time, about 45 minutes. (Placing it on the rack rather than a baking pan will allow the eggplant to roast, rather than steam.)

Remove from the oven, slice the eggplant in half and remove only the softest pulp. Discard the seeds, any tough pulp at the narrow end of the eggplant, and the skin.

In a large skillet, heat 2 tablespoons olive oil until hot but not smoking. Add the eggplant pulp, minced garlic, and thyme. With a whisk (to add air to the mixture and fluff it), whisk regularly over moderate heat until meltingly tender, about 10 minutes. Season with salt, pepper and curry.

Transfer the eggplant "caviar" to a small bowl. Place that bowl in a larger bowl filled with ice, to allow the mixture to cool down quickly. Once completely cooled, whisk in the mayonnaise. Set aside.

Slice the baby eggplants into paper thin, 1/8-inch (2.5 mm) rounds.

Pour the peanut oil into a heavy-duty saucepan. Place a deep-fry thermometer in the oil and heat the oil to 320° F (160° C).

Place the eggplant in a small colander, toss with the flour, shake off any excess and fry until golden, about 3 minutes. With a wire skimmer, lift the eggplant from the oil, and drain. Season with sea salt. Set aside.

Cut each mushroom lengthwise into 1/8-inch (2.5 mm) slices. Brush both sides of each mushroom slice with oil. Season with salt, pepper, and thyme. (Plan on about 14 mushroom slices per serving.)

Preheat a gas, electric, or a ridged, cast-iron, stove top grill. Or prepare a wood or charcoal fire. The fire is ready when the coals glow red and are covered with ash.

SPECIAL MATERIAL
- One 2-inch (5 cm) round pastry cutter
- One 4-inch (10 cm) round pastry cutter

● Select firm, fresh vegetables for the best results.

● Make incisions at regular intervals using a small knife.

● Fill each incision with a garlic sliver.

● Cooking the eggplants on a rack in the oven gives them a roasted flavor.

● Remove all of the pulp from the eggplants, discarding the seeds.

● Whisk the eggplant "caviar" thoroughly to make it meltingly tender.

● Add the mayonnaise to the "caviar" and whisk to lighten the mixture.

● Slice the baby eggplants into paper thin, 1/8-inch (2.5 mm) rounds.

Place each mushroom on the grill at a 45° angle to the ridges of the grill. Grill for 1 minute, pressing firmly down on the mushrooms with a baking sheet, to accentuate the impression of the grill marks. Still grilling the same side of the mushroom, reposition each mushroom at the alternate 45° angle. Grill for 1 minute more, pressing firmly down on the mushrooms with a baking sheet. (This will form a very even and attractive grill mark on the mushrooms.)

Turn each mushroom over and grill on the other side, positioning the mushrooms again at the two angles, pressing firmly down on the mushrooms with a baking sheet, grilling for a total of 2 minutes more.

● Remove the rounds of fried eggplant after they have cooked for about 3 minutes.

● Cut the mushrooms into uniform slices about 1/8-inch (2.5 mm) thick.

● Brush the mushrooms with peanut oil and sprinkle with thyme.

● Season both sides of the mushroom slices with salt and pepper.

Meanwhile, in a large skillet, heat the butter over moderate heat until it sizzles. Add the grilled mushrooms in several carefully arranged layers, sprinkle with thyme and finish cooking, covered, until soft and tender, about 5 minutes more. Do not turn the mushrooms, but rather baste regularly with the buttery cooking juices.

To serve: center a 4-inch (10 cm) round pastry cutter circle on a plate. Using the pastry cutter as a guide, arrange a circle of slightly overlapping slices of mushroom within the cutter, with the "head" or the upper part of each mushroom facing the exterior of the plate. Center a 2-inch (5 cm) round pastry cutter on top of the mushrooms and fill with several tablespoons of eggplant caviar. Remove the cutters from the plate and arrange the rounds of fried eggplant on top of the caviar. Repeat for the remaining 3 servings. At the last minute, place a few grains of coarse sea salt on the fried eggplant rounds. Serve.

Wine suggestion: from the Jura, a light and tasty white Arbois.

● Reposition the mushroom slices during the grilling to give them an attractive grill mark.

● Using a pastry cutter as a guide, arrange the mushrooms in a circle.

● Top the mushrooms with a mound of eggplant "caviar."

● Decorate the "caviar" with the rounds of fried eggplant.

66 THE CÈPE'S DELICATE FLAVOR AND CHARM MANAGES TO ENRICH ALL PREPARATIONS. WITH ITS MEATY TEXTURE AND UNIQUE FLAVOR, THE CÈPE IS THE KING OF MUSHROOMS. 99

SUMMARY

1 ● CÈPE TERRINE WITH SCRAMBLED EGGS
  ● Dominique Bouchet

2 ● ROASTED MONKFISH WITH SMOKED SALT AND CÈPES
  ● Christophe Cussac

3 ● SAUTÉED CÈPES WITH SERANO HAM
  ● Philippe Groult

4 ● WILD MUSHROOM AND DUCK CONFITS TARTS
  ● Benoît Guichard

5 ● SLICED CÈPES WITH ABALONE
  ● Maurice Guillouët

● Joël Robuchon ●

With his "Cèpes grillés au thym et caviar d'aubergines," Joël Robuchon lays out a circle of grilled cèpes, topping them with a velvety caviar of eggplant. The smoky flavor of the eggplant responds naturally to the lightly smoky flavor of grilled mushrooms, illustrating again his theory of parallel flavors. The presentation in the form of tiny circles is reminiscent of the style of presentations from the early days of Jamin.

● Dominique Bouchet ●

Dominique Bouchet once again displays his sense of independence and his own developed style with his "Terrine de cèpes aux œufs battus." What's more, he is the only pupil of five who chose not to slice or grill the cèpes! Presented in a terrine with scrambled eggs, the cèpes are given center stage, with the eggs providing an extra rich taste. But the plate reveals an influence: to catch the eye, the terrine slice is surrounded by small potato rounds, each one topped with a small chive. An aesthetic touch reminiscent of his master.

● Christophe Cussac ●

Christophe Cussac's "Lotte rôtie au sel fumé et concassée de cèpes aux herbes" pairs the hazelnut-like flavor of the cèpe mushroom with the delicate taste of monkfish. But the smoky essence and flavor of the cèpe are underlined by a gentle dose of smoked salt. The simple presentation – rounds of mushrooms flattened out in a circular bed – evokes one of Joël Robuchon's favorite themes, that of the galette or tiny round tart. Christophe Cussac moves away from a strict presentation by arranging the fillets of fish in a cross, one on top of the other, avoiding excessive elaboration.

● Benoît Guichard ●

Benoît Guichard shows that he shares his master's fascination for food formed into a circle, with his "Tourtière aux cèpes et canard confit." The meat is not sautéed but rather steamed. The result is a confit that is more moist and less fatty. Benoît Guichard arranges thin, alternating layers of browned cèpes and steamed duck confit, rustic ingredients typical of country cooking to which he adds a touch of nobility. The dish is meticulously presented, with a garnish of Swiss chard balancing the acidity, and the crusty skin of duck which adds an indispensable touch of texture.

● Philippe Groult ●

Philippe Groult offers a modern interpretation of a traditional dish with his "Poêlée de cèpes au jambon Serano." He selects from Spain this incomparable ham, at once salty, sweet and meltingly tender, which he pairs with slices of cèpes. However, the arrangement differs slightly. He pairs thin slices of ham on the edges of the plate with cèpe slices in the center. Following the example of the master, the garnish of hazelnuts and finely chopped parsley not only create a contrast of colors, but adds a particular texture and sensation of freshness.

● Maurice Guillouët ●

Maurice Guillouët also chooses the "galette" presentation, combining several layers of ingredients, pairing the earthy slices of cèpe and the layer of mysterious aroma of the sea. His "Émincé de cèpes aux ormeaux" marries mushrooms and abalone, two ingredients greatly appreciated in Asia, where they are held in the same regard as foie gras is in France. While adding this refreshing Asiatic touch, the dish bears witness to classic French technique: the abalone is cooked in a reduction of white wine, vermouth, sage, basil and thyme.

Cèpe Terrine with Scrambled Eggs

BY DOMINIQUE BOUCHET

In a large skillet heat 1 tablespoon of the hazelnut oil over high heat. When hot but not smoking, add half the minced mushrooms and cook, shaking the pan until lightly colored, 3 to 4 minutes. Drain and season with salt. Repeat with the remaining oil and mushrooms. Set aside.

Prepare the eggs: crack the eggs into a large bowl, and blend with a fork. Season to taste. In the top of a double boiler set over, barely simmering water, melt the butter.

Add the eggs and cook, stirring regularly with a wooden spoon, until the eggs begin to set but remain creamy and moist, about 20 minutes.

Add the truffle and herbs and stir to blend evenly. Taste for seasoning. Transfer to a large bowl and set aside.

In a large, non-stick skillet, melt the remaining butter from the mushrooms over moderate heat. Add the shallots and a pinch of salt and sweat until soft, 3 to 4 minutes. Add the mushrooms and cook, covered, 5 to 8 minutes, until the mushrooms are warmed through, 3 to 4 minutes. Add the mushrooms to the scrambled egg mixture and toss to blend evenly. Taste for seasoning.

Butter the terrine mold and fill with the egg-mushroom mixture. Smooth the top out with the back of a spoon. Cover and refrigerate overnight.

Prepare the garnish: in a large skillet over moderate heat, melt the butter. When it sizzles, add the onions, reduce heat to low, cover, and cook until soft, 15 to 20 minutes. Set aside.

To serve: cut the terrine into eight even slices. Place a slice in the center of each of the eight dinner plates. Arrange five spring onions alongside each slice of terrine. With a tablespoon, form the tomato concassé into quenelles and garnish each plate with one quenelle. Arrange five small sprigs of fresh chives decoratively on each plate. Repeat for the remaining plates. Serve.

8 SERVINGS

THE MUSHROOMS

- 8 ounces (250 g) fresh cèpe mushrooms, washed, stems trimmed, caps and stems minced
- 2 tablespoons hazelnut oil
- 2 small shallots, peeled and minced
- 2 tablespoons (30 g) unsalted butter

THE SCRAMBLED EGGS

- 12 large eggs
- 2 tablespoons (30 g) unsalted butter
- 2 teaspoons minced fresh black truffle
- 1 teaspoon minced chives
- 1 teaspoon minced tarragon
- 1 teaspoon minced chervil
- 1 teaspoon minced flat-leaf parsley

THE GARNISH

- 3 tablespoons (45 g) unsalted butter
- 40 spring onions (oignons nouveaux) peeled
- 8 tablespoons tomato concassé seasoned with fresh thyme
- 20 stems fresh chives, halved

SPECIAL EQUIPMENT

- One 1 quart (1 l) oval or rectangular porcelain or enameled cast iron terrine
- 1 teaspoon unsalted butter

Wine suggestion: a red Bordeaux, such as a young Pomerol.

Roasted Monkfish with Smoked Salt and Cèpes

BY CHRISTOPHE CUSSAC

In a large skillet, heat 3 tablespoons of olive oil until hot but not smoking. Add the cèpes and cook over a medium heat, tossing constantly, 2 minutes. Season lightly. Cut one mushroom cap into four thick slices for the presentation. Finely dice the remaining mushrooms. Set aside.

In a small saucepan, heat 1 tablespoon oil, add the shallot and sweat for 1 minute. Add the diced cèpes and the garlic. Cover and cook for an additional 5 minutes.

Add the fish stock, soy sauce, vinegar and fresh herbs. Reduce the mixture slightly and remove from the heat. Whisk in 2 tablespoons (30 g) of cold butter. Return the pan to low heat, whisking until the butter has melted. Remove from the heat and whisk in the remaining 2 tablespoons of butter. Return the saucepan to a low heat and whisk until the butter has melted. Taste for seasoning. Set aside to keep warm.

Season the monkfish with smoked salt and pepper. In a large skillet, heat 3 tablespoons olive oil over moderate heat until hot but not smoking. Reduce heat and add the monkfish. Sear for 5 to 7 minutes, turning often so they brown evenly on all sides. The cooking time will vary according to the thickness of the fish.

To serve: divide the mushrooms and their sauce among four warmed dinner plates. Cut each piece of monkfish in half and place on top of the cèpes. Decorate with a mushroom slice and fresh thyme. Serve immediately.

4 SERVINGS

- 7 tablespoons extra-virgin olive oil
- 10 ounces (300 g) cèpe mushrooms, cleaned and patted dry
- Sea salt and freshly ground white pepper to taste
- 1 small shallot, peeled and minced
- 1 small clove fresh garlic, peeled, halved, degermed and crushed
- 3 cups (75 cl) fish stock
- 2 tablespoons soy sauce
- 2 teaspoons sherry vinegar
- 2 tablespoons minced, flat-leaf parsley leaves
- 2 tablespoons minced tarragon leaves
- 2 tablespoons minced chervil
- 2 tablespoons thyme leaves
- 4 tablespoons (60 g) unsalted butter
- One 2 1/2 pound (1.5 kg) monkfish, skinned with the central bone removed, cut into four equal pieces
- 1 teaspoon smoked salt and freshly ground white pepper
- 4 sprigs fresh thyme, for garnish

Wine suggestion: a white Burgundy, such as a fresh and fruity Saint Romain.

Sautéed Cèpes with Serano Ham

BY PHILIPPE GROULT

Prepare the sauce: trim off the tips of the stems of each mushroom. Rinse them quickly under cold water and dry with paper towels to remove excess dirt. In a large saucepan, combine the veal stock and the tips over medium high heat. Bring to a boil and remove. Set aside to infuse. After 30 minutes, strain the mixture through a fine-mesh sieve. Taste for seasoning and keep warm.

Prepare the cèpes: separate the heads from the stems. Set aside the heads. Cut the stems into small dice. Set aside.

Prepare the garnish: in a large skillet, combine 1 tablespoon of olive oil and the shallots over moderate heat. Cook, without colorating, for 2 minutes. Add the diced cèpes and stems and brown lightly, tossing constantly, 2 to 3 minutes. Add the diced ham, chorizo, breadcrumbs and thyme at the last minute. With a wooden spoon, stir to blend. Season with salt and pepper. Discard the thyme. Set aside.

Cook the cèpes: in a medium skillet, heat 1 tablespoon olive oil over high heat. When hot, add half the cèpes and cook, shaking the pan, for about 2 minutes, or until lightly browned. Drain and season with salt. Set aside. Repeat for the remaining cèpes, adding fresh oil for the second batch. Set aside.

Prepare the garlic butter: in a small saucepan, combine the shallots and white wine. Cook over moderate heat until the white wine has fully reduced. Set aside to cool. In a small bowl, whisk together the cooked shallots with the garlic and the butter.

Cook the cèpes: season the cèpes with salt and pepper. In a large skillet, heat the garlic butter over moderate heat and add the cèpes. Cook, uncovered, for 3 minutes. Place the cèpes on a flat work surface and cut each cèpe into several thin slices.

To serve: spoon the garnish in the center of each warmed dinner plate. Layer the cèpe slices over and around the garnish. Decorate with the pieces of Serano ham and the hazelnuts. Spoon the veal sauce over the cèpes and decorate with the flat-leaf parsley. Serve immediately.

4 SERVINGS

THE SAUCE

- 12 ounces (375 g) fresh cèpes, cleaned
- 3/4 cup (18.5 cl) reduced veal stock

THE VEGETABLE GARNISH

- One 2 1/2 ounce (75 g) slice ham
  from Bayonne, blanched and diced
- 3 tablespoons (6 cl) extra-virgin olive oil
- 2 small shallots, peeled and minced
- 1 ounce (30 g) spicy chorizo sausage,
  peeled and diced
- 1 ounce (30 g) breadcrumbs
- 3 sprigs fresh thyme

THE GARLIC BUTTER

- 2 small shallots, peeled and minced
- 1/4 cup (6 cl) white wine
- 4 garlic cloves, peeled, blanched and chopped
- 6 tablespoons (3 ounces; 90 g) unsalted
  butter, softened
- 1 small bunch flat-leaf parsley,
  stemmed, washed and chopped

TO FINISH

- 3 1/2 ounces Serano ham on the bone,
  cut into small pieces
- 8 hazelnuts, halved and toasted
- 20 leaves flat-leaf parsley, washed and dried
- Fine sea salt
- Freshly ground pepper

*Wine suggestion: a Spanish wine, such as
a Manzanilla sherry.*

Wild Mushroom and Duck Confit Tart

BY BENOÎT GUICHARD

In a small, non-stick skillet, sweat the onions in 2 tablespoons duck fat with a pinch of salt over low heat for 3 to 4 minutes. Add the Swiss chard ribs. Cover and cook until soft, 15 to 20 minutes. Set aside.

Meanwhile, in another small non-stick skillet, combine the oil, mushroom caps and stems and brown lightly over moderate heat, 3 to 4 minutes. Season with salt and pepper. Transfer to a sieve to drain. Reserve 80 sliced caps for a final garnish. Finely dice the remaining caps so they are the same size as the Swiss chard. Set aside.

Bring 1 quart (1 l) of water to a simmer in the bottom of a steamer. Place the duck on the steaming rack. Place the rack over simmering water, cover, and steam until the duck is very soft and moist, about 15 minutes. Remove the skin from the duck. Cut the skin into fine dice and reserve. With your hands, pull the meat from the bones and separate it into small pieces and put aside.

In a small skillet, combine 2 tablespoons duck fat and the shallots and sweat over a low heat until soft, 4 to 5 minutes. Add the duck meat and the Madeira and cook, covered, over low heat until the flavors are well-blended, 10 to 12 minutes. Add the mushrooms, half the Swiss chard leaves, half the parsley, and half the garlic and stir to blend. Set aside.

Preheat the oven to 350° F (175° C; gas mark 4/5). Butter the interior of 4 stainless circles measuring about 3 inches (7 1/2 cm) in diameter and 2 inches (5 cm) in height. Place a large piece of parchment paper on a baking sheet. Arrange the circles on top of the paper. Fill the interior of each circle with the duck mixture, flattening out with the back of a spoon. Press down on the mixture slightly so it is well molded. Beginning at the outer edge of the circle, arrange about 14 reserved mushroom slices, slightly overlapping, in a clockwise circle on top of the duck mixture. Working in the opposite direction, arrange about 6 more slices in the center, on top of the first layer of mushrooms. Repeat with the remaining 3 tarts.

In a small bowl, combine the remaining garlic and parsley with the thyme and breadcrumbs. Sprinkle this mixture on top of each tart. Place the baking sheet in the center of the oven and bake for 20 minutes. Meanwhile, in a small skillet, sweat the remaining Swiss chard leaves in the remaining 2 tablespoons (30 g) butter over moderate heat, 3 to 4 minutes. Set aside.

In another small non-stick skillet, sauté the reserved duck skin (with no additional fat) over high heat until crispy. Remove from the heat and immediately deglaze with the vinegar. Set aside.

Remove the baking sheet from the oven. With a spatula, carefully remove the tarts from the pan, drain, and place each in the center of a warmed dinner plate. Remove each circle. Alternate the Swiss chard leaves and crispy bits of duck skin around the tarts. Finish with a splash of duck juice and serve.

4 SERVINGS

- 2 spring onions, peeled and minced
- 4 tablespoons duck fat
- Sea salt to taste
- 2 stalks Swiss chard, trimmed and cleaned, green leaves and white ribs separated; leaves quartered, white ribs diced, blanched, and refreshed
- 3 tablespoons extra-virgin olive oil
- 1 pound (500 g) fresh mushrooms (cèpe or portobello), cleaned, caps and stems separated; caps cut lengthwise into 1/8-inch (2.5 mm) slices
- Freshly ground white pepper to taste
- 3 small legs and thighs of duck confit (preserved duck)
- 2 shallots, peeled and minced
- 2 plump, fresh garlic cloves, peeled and minced
- 3 tablespoons Madeira
- 2 teaspoons fresh, flat-leaf parsley, minced
- 1/2 teaspoon fresh thyme leaves
- 4 tablespoons (2 ounces; 60 g) unsalted butter
- 2 tablespoons fine breadcrumbs
- 3 tablespoons best-quality sherry-wine vinegar
- 4 tablespoons duck cooking juices (or substitute poultry stock)

SPECIAL MATERIAL

- 4 stainless steel circles 3 inches by 2 inches

Wine suggestion: a wine from the Southwest, such as a Cahors, full of tannin.

Sliced Cèpes with Abalone

BY MAURICE GUILLOUËT

Prepare the abalone : shell the abalone. Remove and discard the intestines. Place the abalone under cold running water. With a small brush, remove any black spots. Place them on a work surface and slice them into 1/8-inch (2-3 mm) thick slices. Set aside.

Prepare the sauce : in a large saucepan, combine the white wine, Vermouth, chopped herbs, salt and pepper. Cook over moderate heat until reduced by two thirds. Set aside.

Meanwhile, prepare the cèpes : In a skillet, heat 3 tablespoons of olive oil over moderately high heat. When hot, add the cèpes and brown lightly on one side before tossing to brown the other side, 4 or 5 minutes in all. Season lightly. Drain. With a slotted spoon, transfer half the cèpes to a baking dish. Sprinkle with the thyme.

Cover with the remaining cèpes and sprinkle again with thyme. Set aside. Preheat the oven to the lowest possible setting, 200° F (80° C ; gas mark 1).

Prepare the abalone : in a skillet, melt the butter over moderate heat. Add the abalone and cook, stirring constantly, just until heated through, about 45 seconds. Be careful not to overcook. Add the sauce and heat for about 1 minute. Taste for seasoning. Set aside.

Place the cèpes in the center of the oven and heat right through, 5 minutes. To serve : on each warmed dinner plate, arrange the cèpes in a circle in the center. Place the abalone on the top of the cèpes. Sprinkle with parsley and serve.

4 SERVINGS

- 2 abalone, about 10 to 12 ounces
  (300 to 350 g) each

THE SAUCE

- 1/4 cup (6 cl) white wine
- 1/4 cup (6 cl) Noilly Prat (vermouth)
- 4 leaves fresh sage, washed,
  dried and chopped
- 4 leaves fresh basil, washed, dried
  and chopped
- 2 sprigs fresh thyme, washed, stemmed
  and chopped
- 1 bay leaf, chopped
- Fine sea salt
- 1/4 teaspoon coarsely ground white pepper

THE GARNISH

- 8 tablespoons (12.5 cl) extra-virgin olive oil
- 1/2 pound (250 g) medium-size cèpes, cleaned
  and cut lengthwise into slices
  1/4-inch (5mn) thick
- 1 tablespoon fresh thyme, stemmed
- 6 tablespoons (3 ounces; 80 g) butter
- Sea salt
- Freshly ground pepper

TO FINISH

- 1 tablespoon flat-leaf parsley, washed
  and stemmed

*Wine suggestion: a White from Alsace, such as a
Tokay pinot gris.*

Truffled Sweetbreads with Romaine Lettuce and Herbal Cream Sauce

BY JOËL ROBUCHON

4 SERVINGS

INGREDIENTS
- 4 veal sweetbreads
  (each weighing about
  8 ounces; 250 g)
- 3 ounces (90 g) trimmed fresh
  black truffle
- 4 tablespoons (2 ounces; 60 g)
  unsalted butter
- Fine sea salt
- Coarse sea salt
- Freshly ground black pepper
- 1/2 cup (12.5 cl) chicken or
  veal stock

Soak the sweetbreads: to remove excess blood, soak sweetbreads in several changes of cold water, until the water remains clear, 4 to 5 hours. Drain.

Blanch the sweetbreads: place the soaked and drained sweetbreads in a large saucepan and cover with cold water. Add 1 teaspoon of salt. Bring to a boil and cook for 4 minutes. Remove from the heat and place the casserole containing both the sweetbreads and the liquid in a sink under cold running water. Allow the water to run over the sweetbreads in the pan for 10 minutes, to thoroughly rinse them. Drain.

Trim the sweetbreads: with your fingers, remove the membrane that covers each sweetbread, as well as the fat and tubes attached to the membrane. Set aside.

Cut the whole truffle into matchstick-size julienne. (You should have at least 32 pieces.) Refrigerate.

Trim each leaf of lettuce lengthwise into even rectangles measuring 4 inches by 2 inches (10 cm by 5 cm), making sure the white rib of the lettuce is evenly centered in each small piece.

Fill a large pot with 3 quarts (3 l) of water and bring to a boil over high heat. When the water has come to a boil, add 2 tablespoons of sea salt and the trimmed lettuce leaves. Blanch, uncovered, just until the leaves are softened, about 1 minute. Immediately drain the lettuce leaves and plunge them into cold water to cool down as quickly as possible. Transfer the leaves to a clean towel to dry. Set aside.

With a small knife, make 8 incisions at regular intervals in the sweetbread, and fill each incision with a julienne of truffle. Repeat with the other 3 sweetbreads. Season each sweetbread lightly with salt and pepper.

Garnish
- **24 large leaves Romaine lettuce**
- **3/4 cup (18.5 cl) heavy cream**
- **2 teaspoons finely chopped fresh tarragon leaves**
- **2 teaspoons finely chopped fresh summer savory leaves (or substitute fresh thyme leaves)**
- **2 teaspoons finely minced fresh truffle**

● Rinse the sweetbreads under cold running water for 10 minutes.

● After blanching, remove the membrane that covers each sweetbread.

● Cut the truffle into matchstick-size julienne.

● Trim the edges of the Romaine leaves, making sure the white rib is centered.

● Blanch the Romaine to soften the leaves and rinse under cold water.

● Stud the sweetbreads with the truffle julienne using a small knife or larding needle.

● Place the sweetbreads in the butter as soon as it begins to sizzle.

● Turn them with a spatula and cook until they are evenly browned.

In a large skillet over moderate heat, heat the butter just until it begins to sizzle. (It should not brown or smoke.) Reduce the heat to low and add the sweetbreads. Cook, uncovered, until lightly browned, about 4 minutes per side. With a large spoon, regularly baste the sweetbreads with the juices. (The butter and juices should sizzle very slightly.) Transfer the sweetbreads to a flat rack to drain. Season again with salt and pepper.

Return the skillet with the sweetbread cooking juices to the stove. Over high heat, deglaze the cooking juices with the chicken stock and cook for 2 to 3 minutes. Taste for seasoning. Cover and set aside to keep warm.

● Season again with salt and pepper after the cooking.

● Finely chop the remaining truffle slices.

● Add the chopped truffle to the cream.

● Warm the cream over low heat.

In a large skillet, warm the cream over low heat.

Add the herbs and truffle. In a single layer, add the pieces of lettuce. Cook just long enough to warm the leaves, about 1 minute. Taste for seasoning.

To serve: arrange the 8 rectangles of lettuce in a fan shape in the upper area of a large, warmed dinner plate. Spoon the cream sauce over the lettuce. Place a sweetbread in the lower area of the plate and drizzle with the cooking juices. Repeat for the remaining three plates. Serve immediately.

PRESENTATION OF THE SWEETBREADS
If you prefer to present the sweetbreads in slices, place them on a work surface and use a large, sharp knife to cut into 3 or 4 thick slices. Place the slices on the edge of a plate, overlapping them slightly. Spoon the sauce over them and serve immediately.

Wine suggestion: a red Burgundy, preferably a Volnay of excellent vintage.

● Add the Romaine leaves in a single layer.

● Turn them to coat well with the cream.

● Arrange the Romaine and the sweetbreads side by side on a serving plate.

● Spoon the cream sauce over the lettuce leaves.

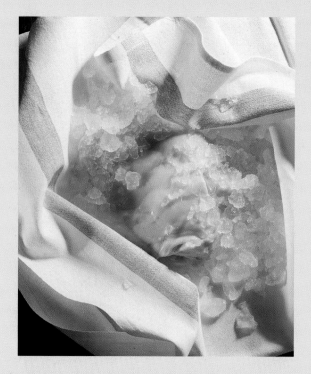

❝ It is the most delicate morsel of the organ meats. Its texture enriches and reinforces the flavor of other ingredients: butter, truffles, fresh herbs, mushrooms. ❞

SUMMARY

1● SALAD OF SWEETBREADS
WITH ROMAINE LETTUCE
● Dominique Bouchet

2● SWEETBREADS WITH FAVA BEANS AND
SUMMER SAVORY
● Christophe Cussac

3● WHOLE SWEETBREADS WITH CABBAGE
AND NUTS
● Philippe Groult

4● SWEETBREADS WITH MORELS AND
NEW BABY ONIONS
● Benoît Guichard

5● SWEETBREADS WITH ARTICHOKES AND
JERUSALEM ARICHOKES CHIPS
● Maurice Guillouët

● Joël Robuchon ●

Browned sweetbreads studded with black truffles, accompanied by crispy pieces of romaine bathed in truffle and cream: Joël Robuchon's "Ris de veau aux truffes et tiges de romaine" combines the best of all worlds. Though sweetbreads hold the center stage in this dish, the aroma of truffle permeates every element, and the texture is dominated by the contrast between the cripsy romaine and the tender sweetbreads. An eye-pleasing medley of green romaine and golden-brown sweetbread. The romaine provides color contrast and acidity.

● Dominique Bouchet ●

Dominique Bouchet must have had a similar concept in mind for his dish. His "Salade de ris de veau aux asperges vertes" pairs pan-seared slices of sweetbread colored in peanut oil with bright green asparagus tossed in raspberry vinaigrette, an acidic and colorful garnish that echoes Robuchon's romaine.

•Christophe Cussac•

With his "Ris de veau aux fèves et à la sariette," Christophe Cussac follows the same theme as his master. The summer savory adds another dimension to the sweetness of fava beans, and the rich green color of the garnish brings out the golden-brown of the sweetbreads. The contrast of textures is appealing, with the melting tenderness of the sweet-breads set against the crunch of the fava beans. At the same time, the palate is awakened by the sharpness of the summer savory.

•Benoît Guichard•

Benoît Guichard takes a more classical approach. His "Ris de veau aux morilles et petits oignons nouveaux", does not center itself on texture, but more on a marriage of sweetbreads with the noble and earthy flavors of morel mushrooms. The cream – a classic partner to morel mushrooms – manages to fix the flavors of the mushroom, all the while adding that essential point of acidity. Harking back to the connection Joël Robuchon established between the earthy truffle and sweetbread, Benoît Guichard follows the same example in his choice of products for this dish.

•Philippe Groult•

Philippe Groult's "Pommes de ris de veau des mendiants aux choux" presents the sweetbreads in the center of cabbage leaves like a delicate flower. The green and gold play nicely off one another, but the touch of genius comes from the blend of nuts sprinkled on top of the meat. As Joël Robuchon likes to say: "The garnish should not only be beautiful, it should also have a function." In effect, the dried nuts and fruits add a crispy texture and evoke the rich, buttery essence of the sweetbreads.

•Maurice Guillouët•

Maurice Guillouët plays with texture in his "Escalopes de ris de veau aux chips de topinambours et artichauts." The sweetbreads, arranged on a bed of cooked artichoke, are topped with crispy chips of Jerusalem artichoke. The brilliant association of the two artichokes permeates the dish, and the crunchy chips serve as a crispy, refreshing touch reminiscent of Robuchon's choice of romaine.

Salad of Sweetbreads and Asparagus

BY DOMINIQUE BOUCHET

Soak the sweetbreads: to remove excess blood, soak the sweetbreads in several changes of cold water, until the water remains clear, 4 to 5 hours. Drain.

Blanch the sweetbreads: place the sweetbreads in a large saucepan and cover with cold water. Add 1 teaspoon salt. Bring to a boil and simmer for 4 minutes. Remove from the heat and place the saucepan containing both the sweetbreads and the liquid in a sink under cold running water. Allow the water to run over the sweetbreads in the pan for 10 minutes, to thoroughly rinse them.

Trim the sweetbreads: with your fingers, remove the membrane that covers each sweetbread, as well as the fat and tubes attached to the membrane. Set aside.

Prepare the vinaigrette: in a small bowl, whisk together the vinegar, the raspberry juice and salt. Add the oil in a thin stream, whisking until well blended. Season with pepper to taste. Stir to blend. Set aside.

Cook the asparagus: prepare a large bowl of ice water. Bring a large pot of water to a boil over a high heat. Add 1 tablespoon salt per quart (liter) of water. After reaching a boil, add the asparagus and cook until tender. Cook until tender, about 5 minutes. With a slotted spoon, transfer to the ice water to cool thoroughly. Drain the asparagus and cut off each end at an angle. Place the asparagus in a single layer on a dish and coat generously with half of the vinaigrette. Set aside.

Cook the sweetbreads: cut the sweetbreads into 1/4-inch thick slices. In a large skillet, heat the peanut oil over moderate heat, just until it sizzles. Season the sweetbread slices with salt and pepper and cook them gently, 3 to 4 minutes on each side, turning once. In a large, non-stick skillet, heat the butter over moderately high heat until it sizzles. Add the mushrooms and toss, cooking until soft, 3 to 4 minutes. Drain and toss with the remaining vinaigrette.

To serve, arrange the slices of sweetbread in the center of each of four warmed dinner plates. Arrange the mushrooms around the sweetbread. Carefully arrange six spears of asparagus — spear end toward the center — like spokes of a wheel on top of the sweetbreads. Arrange a single parsley leaf between each "spoke of the wheel." Repeat for the remaining three servings. Serve immediately.

4 SERVINGS

THE SWEETBREADS

- 12 ounces (360 g) sweetbreads
- 1 tablespoon peanut oil
- 2 small shallots, peeled and minced

THE VINAIGRETTE

- 1 tablespoon best-quality red wine vinegar
- 1 teaspoon raspberry juice
- Sea salt to taste
- 4 tablespoons extra-virgin olive oil
- Freshly ground white pepper to taste

THE ASPARAGUS

- 24 small green asparagus, tough ends trimmed
- 8 ounces (250 g) wild girolle mushrooms, trimmed and cleaned
- 3 tablespoons unsalted butter
- 24 leaves flat-leaf parsley

Wine suggestion: a white from the Languedoc, such as Minervois.

Sweetbreads with Fava Beans and Summer Savory

BY CHRISTOPHE CUSSAC

Soak the sweetbreads in several changes of cold water, until the water remains clear, 4 to 5 hours. Drain. Place the sweetbreads in a large saucepan and cover with cold water. Add 1 teaspoon salt. Bring to a boil over high heat then reduce to a simmer for 1 minute.

Remove from the heat and place the saucepan containing both the sweetbreads and the liquid in the sink under cold, running water. Allow the water to run over the sweetbreads in the pan for 10 minutes, to thoroughly rinse them. Drain. With your fingers, remove the outer membrane that covers each sweetbread, as well as the fat and tubes attached to the membrane. Press the sweetbreads between two plates with a weight on top. Set aside.

Prepare the fava beans: prepare a large bowl of ice water. Bring a large pot of water to a boil, adding 1 tablespoon of salt per quart (liter) of water. Add the beans and cook for 30 seconds. Remove the beans with a slotted spoon, and plunge them into the ice water to cool. Drain. Peel off and discard the tough outer coating as well as the germ. Set aside.

Preheat the oven to 450° F (gas mark 9; 230° C). In a large skillet, heat the butter over medium heat. Season the sweetbreads with salt and white pepper and add them to the skillet. Sauté, to lightly brown them, basting from time to time, 3 to 4 minutes. Add the celery, carrots and onions and sweat for an additional minute. Add the white wine and reduce, uncovered, for 1 minute. Add the veal stock, garlic, 6 leaves of savory and the bouquet garni. Place the skillet in the center of the oven for 10 minutes, basting the sweetbreads frequently as they cook.

Drain the sweetbreads and place in a large ovenproof skillet. Pass the sauce through a fine mesh sieve over the meat and add the fava beans. Taste for seasoning. Place in the center of the oven for an additional 2 minutes, basting so the sweetbreads have a nice brown color.

To serve: arrange the fava beans and sauce on warmed dinner plates. Place the sweetbreads on top. Finish with one savory leaf on each serving for decoration.

4 SERVINGS

- 2 pounds (500 g) veal sweetbreads, each morsel weighing about 1/4 pound
- 4 pounds (2 kg) fresh fava beans, shelled
- Sea salt to taste
- Freshly ground white pepper to taste
- 2 tablespoons (30 g) unsalted butter
- 2 branches celery, washed and finely diced
- 2 carrots, peeled and finely diced
- 2 onions, peeled and finely diced
- 3 tablespoons white wine
- 1 2/3 cups (40 cl) veal stock
- 10 leaves fresh savory, 4 reserved for presentation
- Bouquet garni

Wine suggestion: one of the best red wines of the Hérault, a Faugères.

Whole Sweetbreads with Cabbage and Nuts

BY PHILIPPE GROULT

Prepare the sweetbreads: the day before, prepare a large bowl and combine the water, vinegar and ice cubes. Place the sweetbreads in the mixture until the water remains clear, 18 to 24 hours. Drain.

Place the sweetbreads in a large saucepan. Cover with cold water and add 1 teaspoon of salt. Bring to a boil over high heat. Reduce to a simmer for 2 minutes. Remove from the heat and place saucepan with the sweetbreads under cold water for about 10 minutes to thoroughly rinse. Remove the membrane from around the sweetbreads, and the fat and tubes attached to the membrane. Set cleaned sweetbreads aside.

Pour the white wine into a small saucepan and bring to a boil over high heat. Reduce by half. Set aside. In a small bowl, combine the pine nuts, walnuts, hazelnuts, almonds, pistachios and raisins. Toss to blend. Set aside.

Preheat the oven to 325° F (165° C; gas mark 4). In a large ovenproof skillet, heat 2 tablespoons of olive oil over medium heat until hot but not smoking. Add the carrot, onion and celery and cook, without browning, for about 3 minutes. Add the veal stock, the reduced white wine and the bouquet garni. Cook for an additional 2 minutes.

Arrange the sweetbreads in the skillet. Place the skillet in the oven and cook for 18 minutes. Remove the sweetbreads and drain, reserving the liquids. Strain the cooking liquid through a fine-mesh sieve set over a clean saucepan. Reserve the vegetables.

Bring the liquid to a boil over high heat. Reduce the heat and reduce the liquid by half. Set aside. Cook the cabbage: prepare a large bowl of ice water. Bring a large pot of water to a boil. Add 1 tablespoon salt per quart (liter) of water and add the cabbage leaves. Cook until tender, about 4 minutes. With a slotted spoon remove the cabbage and transfer to the ice water. Once cooled, drain and set aside.

In a large skillet, combine the peanut oil and 3 tablespoons butter over high heat. Add the sweetbreads and cook, turning frequently, until they are thoroughly browned and crispy on all sides. Add the lemon gelatin and baste the sweetbreads, coating them thoroughly with the gelatin. Remove. Place the sweetbreads in a pan and sprinkle the nut mixture over them. Set aside.

Prepare the sauce: deglaze the skillet with all but 4 tablespoons of the reduced cooking liquid. Reduce until the sauce is thick and syrupy. Add the reserved vegetables. Taste for seasoning. Set aside. Prepare the cabbage: in a medium saucepan, heat the remaining 4 tablespoons of cooking liquid. When hot, add the remaining 3 tablespoons (45 g) of butter and whisk to blend. Add the cabbage leaves and heat just to warm through, stirring gently, 2 to 3 minutes. Add the truffles (if using). Taste for seasoning.

To serve: sprinkle the remaining olive oil over the sweetbreads. Arrange 6 cabbage leaves in the center of 4 warmed dinner plates. Place the sweetbread in the center of the cabbage leaves. Sprinkle the nuts over the meat. Spoon the vegetables and sauce over and around the sweetbreads and onto each plate. Serve immediately.

4 SERVINGS

- 1 cup (25 cl) water
- 1 cups (31 cl) distilled white vinegar
- 10 large ice cubes
- 4 veal sweetbreads, each weighing 7 ounces (200 g)
- 1 cup (37.5 cl) white wine

MIXED NUT GARNISH

- 12 pine nuts
- 4 walnuts, shelled and halved
- 8 hazlenuts, shelled and halved
- 8 almonds, shelled and skinned
- 8 pistachios, shelled and skinned
- 12 golden raisins

- 3 tablespoons extra-virgin olive oil
- 1 carrot, washed, peeled and finely diced
- 1 onion, peeled and finely diced
- 1 stalk of celery, washed and finely diced
- 2 cups (50 cl) veal stock
- Bouquet garni: several parsley stems, celery leaves and sprigs of fresh thyme, wrapped in the green part of a leek and securely tied with cotton twine
- 24 baby cabbage leaves, washed
- 2 tablespoons peanut oil
- 6 tablespoons (3 ounces; 90 g) unsalted butter
- 1 teaspoon lemon gelatin powder
- 1 ounce (30 g) fresh black truffle, finely diced (optional)

Wine suggestion: a Burgundy, such as a red Savigny-lès-Beaune from an excellent year.

Sweetbreads with Morels and New Baby Onions

BY BENOÎT GUICHARD

Soak the sweetbreads: to remove excess blood, soak sweetbreads in several changes of cold water, until the water remains clear, 4 to 5 hours. Drain.

Blanch the sweetbreads: place the soaked and drained sweetbreads in a large saucepan and cover with cold water. Add 1 teaspoon of salt. Bring to a boil and simmer for 4 minutes, counting from the time the water comes back to a simmer. Remove from the heat and place the casserole containing both the sweetbreads and the liquid in a sink under cold running water. Allow the water to run over the sweetbreads in the pan for 10 minutes, to thoroughly rinse them. Drain.

Trim the sweetbreads: with your fingers, remove the membrane that covers each sweetbread, as well as the fat and tubes attached to the membrane. Set aside.

In a large saucepan, combine 3 tablespoons of butter, the onions, a pinch of fine salt and the sugar. Cover and cook over low heat until soft and confit-like, 25 to 30 minutes. Set aside.

In a small saucepan, combine 1 tablespoon (1/2 ounce; 15 g) unsalted butter and the shallot. Sweat, covered, over low heat, cooking just until the shallot is softened, 2 to 3 minutes. The shallot should not brown. Set aside.

Trim the morels and rinse quickly under cold running water. Drain thoroughly. Halve each mushroom lengthwise. Set aside.

In a large skillet, heat 5 tablespoons (2 1/2 ounces; 75 g) butter over moderate heat, just until it sizzles. Add the morels, cover, and cook gently for about 15 minutes. Add the shallot, cream and chervil. Taste for seasoning. Set aside and keep warm.

Cut the sweetbreads into slices 1/4-inch (5 mm) thick. In a large skillet, heat the remaining 5 tablespoons (2 1/2 ounces; 75 g) butter over moderate heat, just until it sizzles. Season the sweetbread slices with salt and pepper and cook them gently, 3 to 4 minutes per side, turning once.

To serve: in the center of each of four large, warm dinner plates, arrange several overlapping slices of sweetbread. Spoon the reduced veal stock over and around the sweetbreads. Spoon the morels over the sweetbreads. Garnish with parsley and chives. Serve immediately.

4 SERVINGS

- 2 veal sweetbreads (each weighing about 8 ounces; 250 g)
- Sea salt to taste
- 14 tablespoons (7 ounces: 200 g) unsalted butter
- 20 spring onions, peeled
- A pinch of sugar
- 1 shallot, peeled
- 12 ounces (375 g) fresh morel mushrooms
- 1 tablespoon crème fraîche or heavy cream
- 1 tablespoon fresh, minced chervil leaves
- 6 tablespoons (1 dl) reduced veal stock (optional), warmed
- Fresh minced chives, chopped, for garnish
- Several fresh flat-leaf parsley leaves

Wine suggestion: a grand and mature Saint-Émilion.

Sweetbreads with Artichokes and Jerusalem Artichokes Chips

BY MAURICE GUILLOUËT

Soak sweetbreads in several changes of cold water, until water remains clear, 18 to 24 hours. Drain.

Place sweetbreads in a large saucepan and cover with cold water. Add 1 teaspoon salt. Bring to boil over high heat. Reduce and cook for 4 minutes, counting from the time the water returns to a boil. Remove, place under cold running water to thoroughly rinse sweetbreads, 10 minutes.

Trim sweetbreads, remove membrane, fat, and tubes attached to the membrane. Set aside.

In a large skillet, combine artichoke, oil and juice of one lemon. Cover with water and cook over moderate heat until just soft, 6 to 8 minutes. Remove from heat and reserve in cooking liquid.

In a small bowl, combine the Jerusalem artichokes, juice of half a lemon and cold water to cover. Soak for 30 minutes. Cut each artichoke into 1/8-inch (3 mm) slices. Dry thoroughly in a thick towel.

Pour the peanut oil into a heavy saucepan. Heat the oil to 280° F (140° C). Fry the Jerusalem artichokes in batches (about 6 slices at a time) until lightly golden, 2 to 3 minutes per batch. With a flat-mesh skimmer, transfer to paper towels to drain.

Sprinkle immediately with salt and pepper. Keep warm.

In a small skillet, heat 1 tablespoon (15 g) butter. Add the shallot and cook over moderate heat, 4 to 5 minutes, without colorating. Season with salt and pepper. Set aside.

Drain artichoke hearts and discard the cooking liquid. Heat 3 table-spoons (45 g) butter over moderate heat. Add artichoke hearts and toss to coat with the butter. Add the shallot. Season with salt and pepper. Just before serving, blend in the chopped parsley. Set aside.

Cut sweetbreads into slices 1/4-inch (5 mm) thick. In a large skillet, combine remaining peanut oil and butter over moderate heat, just until it sizzles. Season sweetbread slices with salt and pepper and cook gently, coloring them 3 to 4 minutes on each side, turning once.

In a small saucepan, heat the veal juices until hot, but not boiling. Set aside.

To serve: in the center of each warmed dinner plate, arrange six triangles of artichoke heart in the center. Arrange the slices of sweetbread around them. Spoon the veal juices around the slices and sprinkle with the Jerusalem artichoke chips and the julienned parsley. Serve immediately.

4 SERVINGS

- 2 veal sweetbreads (each weighing about 8 ounces; 250 g)
- 1 teaspoon coarse sea salt
- 4 trimmed artichoke hearts, cut into 6 triangles
- 4 tablespoons extra-virgin olive oil
- Juice 1 1/2 lemons
- 8 ounces (250 g) Jerusalem artichokes, peeled
- 1 1/4 cups (30 cl) peanut oil
- 6 tablespoons (90 g) unsalted butter
- 1 small shallot, peeled and minced
- 2 cups parsley leaves, washed and stemmed, one half julienned, one half finely chopped
- 4 tablespoons veal cooking juices
- Fine sea salt
- Freshly ground pepper

Wine suggestion: a red Bordeaux, such as an elegant Saint-Julien.

GROS

EN GROS

75

- 46000 CAHORS - Tél. 65 22 24 80

TRUFFES
fraiche

M Joël Robuchon
59 Ave R. Poincaré
75 016 PARIS

REMIS le

Truffle, Onion, and Bacon Tartlets

BY JOËL ROBUCHON

4 SERVINGS

INGREDIENTS

- 4 black truffles (each about 1 1/2 ounces; 45 g)
- 1 plump, fresh garlic clove, peeled and halved
- 5 tablespoons goose fat, softened
- 3 sheets phyllo dough
- 3 tablespoons (1 1/2 ounces; 45 g) unsalted butter, softened
- 12 ounces (375 g) dried baby onions, peeled
- 1 plump, fresh garlic clove, finely minced
- 2 to 3 very thin slices bacon (about 2 ounces; 70 g), chilled and cut into thin julienne
- Sea salt and freshly ground white pepper to taste
- 2 teaspoons Madeira
- 3 tablespoons crème fraîche
- Fleur de sel

Trim the truffles. With a mandoline, cut 116 paper-thin slices of truffle. With a 1 1/4-inch (3 cm) cookie cutter, reshape each truffle round to trim away any uneven edges. Reserve all trimmings. Mince and set aside.

Rub each waxed paper disk with the garlic halves. With a brush, generously coat the same side of each paper disk with goose fat.

With a brush, coat both sides of each truffle slice with goose fat. Place 1 truffle slice in the center of a prepared waxed paper disk. Arrange 7 other slices, slightly overlapping, in a clockwise circle around the center truffle. Working in the opposite direction, arrange 14 more slices in another slightly overlapping counter-clockwise circle of truffles. Repeat to make 3 more tart bases. Place a prepared disk of paper, coated side down, on top of each truffle base, pressing down firmly. Refrigerate the tart bases at least 1 hour to harden the goose fat.

Preheat the oven to 400° F (200° C; gas mark 6/7).

Place a sheet of phyllo dough on a non-stick baking sheet. Using a pastry brush, coat lightly with butter. Top with a second sheet of phyllo and coat it lightly with butter too. Top with a third sheet, but do not butter. Place a 5-inch (13 cm) round pastry cutter on top of the phyllo sheets. With a small, sharp knife, use the pastry cutter as a template and cut around the pastry cutter to form a disk of phyllo dough. Repeat for 3 more disks. Weight by placing another baking sheet of the same size on top. (This will prevent the dough from puffing up as it bakes). Place in the center of the oven and bake until light golden, 8 to 10 minutes. Remove from the oven and set aside. Leave the baked phyllo disks on the baking sheet. (Can be prepared up to 1 hour in advance.)

Cut an onion in half lengthwise. Place it cut-side down on a work surface, and cut in thin, almost transparent half-moon slices. Repeat until all the onions are sliced in this manner.

SPECIAL EQUIPMENT
- **Eight 5-inch (13 cm) wax paper disks**

● Cut the truffles into paper-thin slices and trim edges with a cookie cutter.

● Spread out the wax paper disks and rub each with garlic.

● With a brush, generously coat the same side of each disk with goose fat.

● Using a small knife, arrange the truffle slices, slightly overlapping, in a circle.

● Begin by placing 8 truffle slices in the center of each disk.

● Working in the opposite direction, add 14 more truffle slices, overlapping slightly.

● Place another wax paper disk, coated-side down, on top, pressing down firmly.

● Brush a sheet of phyllo dough lightly with butter.

In a large skillet, combine the onions, garlic, a pinch of salt and the remaining goose fat over low heat. Sweat, covered until softened, about 20 minutes. The onions should not brown. Add the bacon and the truffle trimmings and warm over low heat, about 30 seconds. Add the Madeira and cook 2 minutes more, stirring constantly.

Stir in the crème fraîche and cook 2 to 3 minutes more. Taste for seasoning adding additional salt and pepper as necessary.

● Top with a second and third sheet of phyllo dough.

● Cut out circles of phyllo dough using a pastry cutter.

● The phyllo dough should be lightly browned.

● Add the bacon and truffle trimmings to the onion mixture.

To assemble the tarts: Evenly spread the onion mixture on top of the phyllo disks on the baking sheet. Remove the truffle bases from the refrigerator, peal away the top piece of paper and turn out onto the onion mixture. Leave the top paper round intact. Return the baking sheet to the oven for 1 minute, or just long enough to melt the fat that is holding the truffles together.

Remove from the oven as soon as the fat melts. With a spatula, carefully transfer each tart to a warmed dinner plate. Gently peel away and discard the top layer of paper. Sprinkle with fleur de sel and pepper.

Wine suggestion: a white from the northern Rhone valley, such as an Hermitage from a very good year.

● Spread the onion mixture evenly over the top of the phyllo disks.

● Invert the truffle rounds onto the onion mixture, removing the base but leaving the top paper.

● Carefully peel away and discard the top layer of paper.

● Place the tartlet on a plate and sprinkle with a pinch of fleur de sel and pepper.

66 FEW INGREDIENTS CAN HOLD SUCH A FESTIVAL OF FLAVORS FOR ALL THE SENSES — OFFERING TEXTURE, AROMA, SIMPLICITY AND PURE ESSENCE. 99

SUMMARY

●

● Joël Robuchon ●

With his "Tarte friande aux truffes, oignons et lard fumé," Joël Robuchon employs a simple tart, delicately perfumed with bacon and onions, as the backdrop for the truffle. Simple and elegant, the tart is a classical foundation for celebrating the deep, exquisite flavor of the truffle as the primary ingredient in the dish.

● Dominique Bouchet ●

Dominique Bouchet displays his independence and creativity by opting for the very delicately perfumed white truffle. Using a classic brandade of fresh cod as a model, his "Brandade de morue aux truffes blanches" marries the simplicity of potatoes with the flavors of the ocean, and perfumes the ensemble with shavings of fresh white truffles.

● Christophe Cussac ●

Christophe Cussac employs one of the most classical dishes of all for his backdrop: pot-au-feu. His dish, "Pot-au-feu de foie gras en paysanne truffée" is a simple duck bouillon with poached foie gras speckled with chopped truffle. The sheer simplicity of the dish leaves ample space for the truffle to shine and take center stage.

● Benoît Guichard ●

Benoît Guichard also opts for a simple backdrop, rolling chicken meat and duxelles of white mushrooms into his "Cannellonis aux truffes fraîches." With chopped truffles in the mushroom stuffing and thick slices of truffle underneath the cannelloni, the dish is dominated by their earthy flavor.

● Philippe Groult ●

Philippe Groult uses a solid foundation with a familiar theme for his truffle dish. His "Fumet de truffe en gelée" layers veal gelée with diced vegetables and truffles, and coats it with a layer of fois gras cream decorated with truffle slices. The dish is very complex, but entirely reminiscent of Robuchon's "Gelée de caviar, crème de chou-fleur." Visually, it is a perfect example of a dish created in the style of Joël Robuchon.

● Maurice Guillouët ●

Maurice Guillouët follows the example of his master in terms of pure simplicity. With his "Croustillant de langoustines aux truffes," he takes fresh langoustines cooked in goose fat (a method used by Robuchon in the early days of Jamin), sprinkles them with truffles and sandwiches them between two layers of buckwheat galettes flavored with chopped truffle. Following his master's example, Maurice Guillouët exploits the other elements in the dish – buckwheat galettes and langoustines from his native Brittany – to enhance the flavor and essence of the black truffle.

Brandade of Fresh Cod with White Truffles

BY DOMINIQUE BOUCHET

Prepare the potato puree: scrub the potatoes, but do not peel them. Place the potatoes in a medium-size saucepan, add salted water (1 tablespoon salt per quart (liter) of water) to cover. Simmer, uncovered, over moderate heat until a knife inserted into a potato comes away easily, 20 to 30 minutes. Drain the potatoes as soon as they are cooked.

As soon as the potatoes are cool enough to handle, peel them. Pass through the finest grid of a food mill into a medium-size bowl. Set aside.

In a large saucepan, combine the cream and the cod. Wrap the garlic, bay leaf, thyme and peppercorns in a small piece of cheesecloth and tie in a bundle. Add the herb bundle to the saucepan. Bring the cream just to a boil over medium heat. Lower the heat and simmer, 12 to 15 minutes. Drain the fish. Do not discard the cooking liquid. Place the cod in a food processor, and blend slightly, pulsing on and off.

Transfer the cod to the potato puree and add enough cooking liquid to obtain a smooth mixture. Taste for seasoning. Set aside.

Prepare the lemon sections: cut both ends off 1 lemon. Place the lemon, cut end down, on a work surface. With a small sharp knife, slice off a strip of peel cutting downward, following the curve of the lemon. All of the pith (the white part) should be removed, leaving only the fruit. Continue cutting away strips of peel with the pith until it is completely removed. To separate and lift out each lemon section, begin by slicing between the membrane and the fruit of 1 section, and carefully lift it out. Move to the next lemon section, and slice between the membrane and the fruit. Use the knife to gently ease the fruit away from the other membrane(the one that was attached to the first section removed), taking care to keep the section intact. Reserve the clean lemon sections in a small bowl. When finished, place the lemon sections on a work surface and quarter them into cubes. Remove any unwanted seeds. Set aside.

With a truffle slicer or mandoline, cut the truffle into 48 thin slices. Mince any remaining truffle. Set aside.

In a small bowl, combine the oil, lemon sections, chives, tomato, and minced truffle. Toss to blend. Taste for seasoning. Set aside.

To serve: place three quenelles of the brandade in the center of each plate. Stand four slices of truffle on end in the quenelles. Spoon three tiny mound of the tomato and lemon mixture around the brandade. Serve with grilled country bread.

4 SERVINGS

- 8 ounces (250 g) small yellow-fleshed potatoes, such as the ratte variety
- 4 tablespoons heavy cream
- 3/4 pound (375 g) skinned fresh cod, diced
- 2 plump, fresh garlic cloves, peeled and finely chopped
- 1 fresh bay leaf
- 1 sprig fresh thyme
- 1 teaspoon whole white peppercorns
- l lemon, preferably organic, washed
- 1 1/2 ounces (45 g) fresh white truffle
- 8 tablespoons extra-virgin olive oil
- 1 tablespoon minced chives
- 1 tomato, peeled, cored, seeded and chopped
- Sea salt and freshly ground white pepper to taste

Wine suggestion: a white from the Rhône valley, such as a fine and delicate Condrieu.

Pot-au-Feu with Foie Gras and "Countryman's" Truffles

BY CHRISTOPHE CUSSAC

Prepare the bouillon: place the duck trimmings in a stockpot and add cold water to cover. Bring to a boil over high heat, skimming impurities that rise to the surface. Add the carrots, celery, onions, garlic clove, bouquet garni and a pinch of coarse salt. Simmer gently for 2 hours. Do not allow the bouillon to reduce too much. Strain and divide the bouillon into two separate containers. Set aside.

Prepare the foie gras: with the tip of a small, sharp knife, carefully remove any traces of green from the surface of the foie gras. With your hands, separate the larger lobe from the smaller one by gently pulling them apart. Cut each lobe crosswise, making a total of eight 1-inch (2.5 cm) thick slices. Again, with the tip of a small, sharp knife remove the thin, transparent skin surrounding each piece of duck liver. Remove and discard the thin red blood vessel that runs lengthwise through the inside of each lobe. Refrigerate.

Prepare the sauce: in a large saucepan, heat the duck fat over low heat. Add the carrots, celery root, potato and leek and cook for 1 minute. Add half the duck bouillon and cook the vegetables over medium heat for 5 to 8 minutes. The vegetables should be cooked, not crunchy. Strain the bouillon, reserving the vegetables and cooking liquid separately.

In a medium-size saucepan, reduce the remaining bouillon to 3/4 cup (18.5 cl). Add the vegetables and one quarter of the truffles. Set aside, keeping warm.

In a large saucepan, bring the vegetable cooking liquid to a gentle simmer over moderate heat. Lower the foie gras into the bouillon and poach gently for 2 to 3 minutes, maintaining a gentle simmer. Cook until the foie gras begins to melt and is warmed through. Drain.

To serve, divide the vegetable-truffle mixture, and its liquid, among four warmed, shallow soup bowls. Set two pieces of foie gras in the bouillon. Sprinkle the foie gras with the reserved minced truffles. Sprinkle with coarse salt and cracked white pepper. Serve immediately.

4 SERVINGS

THE BOUILLON

- 2 1/2 pounds (1.5 kg) duck trimmings (necks, wing tips, backs), chopped into small pieces
- 3 medium carrots, peeled
- 2 small branches celery, washed
- 2 medium onions, peeled
- 1 garlic clove, peeled
- Bouquet garni

THE FOIE GRAS

- 1 duck foie gras, 3/4 pound (375 g)

THE SAUCE

- 1 1/2 tablespoons duck fat
- 2 small carrots, peeled and finely diced
- 1/4 celery root, peeled and finely diced
- 1 potato, peeled and finely diced
- 1 leek, white and tender green parts, washed and finely diced
- 1/2 ounce (15 g) fresh black truffle, finely minced
- Coarse salt
- Coarsely ground white pepper (mignonette)

Wine suggestion: a white from Alsace, such as a Tokay pinot gris.

Aspic and Foie Gras with Truffles

BY PHILIPPE GROULT

Prepare the calf's feet: when purchased, a calf's foot generally includes the hoof and the thin upper leg bone enclosed with flesh and skin. To prepare, split them in two. With a sharp boning knife, carve the meat and the skin from the upper leg bone. Reserve all the pieces, including the bone. (Or ask your butcher to do this for you.) Place the pieces of calf's foot and the calf shank in a large stockpot and add cold water to cover. Salt and bring the water to a boil over high heat. Skim any impurities from the top and simmer for 2 minutes. Drain. Return the pieces to the stockpot, add the skin, and rinse under cold, running water for 15 minutes to refresh. Drain.

Cook the jelly: rinse out the stockpot and combine the blanched calf's foot and the shank pieces, the carrot, onion, leek and bouillon cube, 3 tablespoons coarse seas salt, and cover with cold water. Bring to a boil over moderately high heat.

When the water boils, reduce the heat to low and simmer gently for 3 hours, skimming any impurities that may rise to the surface. Line a sieve with moistened cheesecloth. Set the sieve over a large bowl, and ladle – do not pour – the stock into the prepared sieve. Remove the meat and gelatin from the bones. Discard any hard or very firm portions of meat, gristle, or tendon. Discard the bones. Cut or pull the shank meat into small pieces. Set aside. Cut about 1/4 of the meat into a small dice. Set aside to cool and solidify.

Prepare the foie gras cream: in a large bowl, combine all the ingredients and whisk lightly to blend. The mixture should be smooth. Season with salt and pepper. Refrigerate.

Prepare the vegetable garnish: in a large skillet, heat the oil over moderate heat until hot but not smoking. Add the shallots and cook for 2 minutes without coloring. Add the carrots and cook for an additional 3 minutes. With a wooden spoon, blend the vegetables as they cook. Add the celery root, celery, fennel and mushrooms and cook, covered, for 5 minutes more. Add the truffle juice and reduce over moderately high heat, for 2 to 3 minutes.

In a small saucepan, combine the calf's foot jelly and the remaining truffle juice and reheat slightly, just to soften. Divide the vegetable garnish evening into four conical soup bowls. Sprinkle the diced calf's foot and veal shank over the vegetables. Slowly and carefully pour the semi-set jelly over each. The jelly should be syrupy in texture and cold to the touch. Place the bowls in the refrigerator until firm, about 20 minutes. When set, pour an additional 1/2 inch (2.5 cm) layer of jelly over each. Refrigerate for an additional 15 minutes.

To finish: remove the foie gras cream from the refrigerator and mix to blend. Cut 4 small straws to fit the diameter of the bowls. Gently place a straw into surface of the cool jelly in each bowl so it visually cuts the surface in half.

Carefully and slowly, pour a thin layer of the foie gras cream on top of one half of the set jelly. Refrigerate for 15 minutes. Carefully remove the straws.

To serve: decorate the surface of the foie gras cream with the truffle slices, making flower-like designs around the edges and in the center. Serve immediately

4 SERVINGS

THE CALF'S FOOT JELLY

- 2 calf's feet
- 10 ounces (300 g) veal shank, cut into pieces
- 1 carrot, peeled and chopped
- 1 onion, peeled and pierced with 3 cloves
- The green portion of a leek, washed and chopped
- 1 cube instant chicken bouillon
- 6 quarts (6 l) water
- 4 tablespoons (6 cl) truffle juice

THE FOIE GRAS CREAM

- 3 ounces (105 g) fresh duck foie gras, passed through a fine-mesh sieve
- 3 tablespoons heavy cream
- 6 tablespoons (10 cl) calf's foot jelly
- 3 tablespoons white port
- 4 tablespoons (6 cl) truffle juice
- A pinch of freshly ground coriander

THE VEGETABLE GARNISH

- 2 tablespoons extra-virgin olive oil
- 2 small shallots, peeled and minced
- 2 small carrots, peeled and cut into a very small dice
- ounce (15 g) fresh celery root, peeled and finely diced
- 1 stalk fresh celery, washed and finely diced
- bulb fennel, finely diced
- 2 mushrooms, tough ends trimmed, washed and finely diced
- 12 tablespoons (18 cl) truffle juice
- 3 ounces (105 g) fresh truffles (cut into 20 medium-size half moons, 36 small half moons, the remainder finely diced)
- Coarse sea salt
- Fine sea salt
- Freshly ground white pepper

Wine suggestion: a Rhône valley white, such as a Crozes-Hermitage.

Cannellonis with Fresh Truffles

BY BENOÎT GUICHARD

Prepare the chicken garnish: in a large saucepan, combine the chicken wings, water, mushroom stems, leek, fresh ginger and the bouquet garni. Season with coarse sea salt. Add the chicken wings and bring to a simmer over medium high heat. Reduce heat and cook, covered, until the flesh on the wings is tender and almost falls off the bone, 20 to 25 minutes. Reserve the cooking liquid for another use. Drain. Set aside.

Prepare the stuffing: in a medium-size skillet, heat 1 table-spoon (15 g) of butter and sweat the shallots over low heat, stirring constantly, 3 to 5 minutes. Add a pinch of fine sea salt. Set aside. Place the diced mushroom caps in a clean kitchen towel. Wring out any excess water from the mushrooms. In a large casserole, heat 1 tablespoon (15 g) of butter and add half the cooked shallots. Add the mushrooms, cover, and cook over a low heat until soft, 8 to 10 minutes. Add the chopped truffle. Taste for seasoning and cook for an additional 5 to 8 minutes, mixing from time to time. Add the heavy cream and the béchamel sauce. Cook over low heat, stirring constantly, until the mixture is smooth and well-blended, 1 to 2 minutes. Set aside to cool.

Prepare the chicken wings: using a small, sharp knife, remove the skin from the chicken wings. Extract the meat and add to the cooling mushroom stuffing. Discard the bones and skin. Taste for seasoning and set aside.

Prepare the cannelloni: in a small saucepan, add 1 cup (25 cl) heavy cream and bring just to a boil over a high heat. Lower the heat and reduce slightly, 2 to 3 minutes. Set aside. Preheat the broiler. In a large pot, bring 6 quarts of water to a rolling boil over a high heat. Add the salt and the pasta, stirring to keep the pasta from sticking. Cook until tender but firm to the bite, or al dente. Drain thoroughly. Set aside.

Assemble the cannelloni: Place a piece of plastic wrap over a flat work surface. Place a sheet of lasagna on the plastic. Spoon about 3 tablespoons of mushroom stuffing in a thin line, lengthwise, in the center of the sheet. Using the plastic wrap to help you push, roll the pasta up lengthwise, cigar-style, to enclose the stuffing. Once the roll is secure, gently remove the plastic wrap and close the pasta roll completely. The two long edges of the lasagna should be even and tightly-rolled. Trim both edges on an angle. Repeat for the remaining sheets of pasta. Set aside. With a brush, evenly coat the gratin dish with butter. Arrange the cannelloni in the dish, leaving space between each one. Coat each roll with the reduced heavy cream and sprinkle with the cheese. Place the dish about 5 inches (12.5 cm) from the broiler and heat just until slightly browned, 2 to 3 minutes.

Prepare the sauce: add the reserved truffle slices to the skillet containing the remaining cooked shallots. Taste for seasoning. Cover and sweat over low heat for 4 to 5 minutes. Add the port and bring to gentle simmer over a medium heat. Strain the truffle slices through a fine-mesh sieve and pour the liquid into a small saucepan. Reserve the truffle slices. Heat the sauce over low heat and whisk in the 2 tablespoons (30 g) butter. When the butter is incorporated, add the truffle slices and remove from the heat. Taste for seasoning. Place two truffle slices in the center of each plate. Sprinkle each slice with a few drops of lemon juice. Place a cannelloni on top of each truffle round. Spoon the sauce around them and finish with a sprinkling of chives. Serve immediately.

4 SERVINGS

THE CHICKEN GARNISH

- 20 chicken wings
- 1 quart (1 l) water
- 10 ounces (300 g) mushrooms, washed, caps and stems separated (caps reserved for stuffing)
- 1 small leek, washed, white and tender green parts
- 1 ounce (30 g) fresh ginger, peeled and thickly sliced
- Bouquet garni: several parsley stems and sprigs of thyme wrapped in the white part of a leek and securely fastened with a cotton twine
- Coarse sea salt to taste

THE MUSHROOM STUFFING

- 2 tablespoons (30 g) butter
- 6 shallots, peeled and minced
- The reserved mushroom caps, finely diced
- 8 ounces (250 g) fresh truffles (Cut half the truffles into about 8 slices 1/4-inch (1/2 cm) thick. Finely dice the remaining truffles)
- 1 tablespoon heavy cream
- 1 tablespoon béchamel sauce, or substitute an additional tablespoon of heavy cream

THE CANNELLONI

- 1 cup (25 cl) heavy cream
- 8 sheets lasagna, fresh or dried pasta
- 3 tablespoons coarse sea salt
- 1 tablespoon butter (15 g) for the gratin dish
- 1 1/4 cups (about 4 ounces; 100 g) finely grated Gruyère cheese

THE SAUCE

- 1/3 cup (8 cl) good quality Port
- 2 tablespoons (30 g) butter

THE FINISHING TOUCH

- The 8 reserved truffle slices
- 1 tablespoon freshly squeezed lemon juice
- 1 tablespoon fresh, minced chives

Wine suggestion: a mature Côte-rôtie, from the côte brune.

Crispy Pancakes and Langoustines with Truffles

BY MAURICE GUILLOUËT

Prepare the pancake batter: In a medium-size bowl, combine the two kinds of flour with a pinch of salt. Slowly whisk in the egg, whisking until smooth. Add the water and mix to blend. Set aside to rest for 30 to 45 minutes.

Prepare the langoustine bouillon: in a large skillet, heat the olive oil over high heat and sear the langoustine heads, tossing constantly, 4 to 5 minutes. Meanwhile, in a medium-size skillet, heat 1 tablespoon (15 g) butter. Add the shallots and fennel and cook over moderate heat, 3 minutes, without coloring.

Combine the vegetables with the langoustine heads. Add the bouquet garni, tomato concentrate and water. Season. Cook over a medium high heat for 15 minutes, maintaining a steady simmer.

Remove from heat and let it rest 30 minutes before passing through a fine-mesh sieve. Reduce by half. Set aside.

Cook the pancakes: add 1 1/2 ounces (45 g) of the truffles to the batter and whisk to blend. Heat a large skillet over moderate heat and add 1 tablespoon lightly salted butter. With a ladle, add the batter to the pan to make pancakes 4 to 5 inches (10 to 12 1/2 cm) in diameter. Cook the pancakes in batches, counting 2 per person. Set aside.

In a medium-size saucepan, heat 1 tablespoon (15 g) butter and add the celery root and the remaining truffles. Season with salt and pepper and cook, covered, over moderate heat, 2 minutes. Set aside 4 teaspoons of the mixture for presentation.

Add the langoustine bouillon to the remaining vegetables and simmer gently over medium heat, 3 to 5 minutes.

Add 3 tablespoons (45 g) butter and whisk to blend until the butter is fully incorporated. Taste for seasoning. Set aside.

In a large skillet, heat the remaining lightly salted butter until hot. Add the pancakes in batches, and brown lightly in the butter, turning once, 2 minutes on each side. Drain.

Cook the langoustines: in a large skillet, melt the goose fat over high heat. When hot, add the langoustines and cook until slightly firm, 2 to 3 minutes on each side. Season with salt and pepper. Place a pancake on each warmed plate. Arrange 5 langoustines on each cake in a circle. Spoon over the vegetable garnish and the sauce. Cover with a second pancake. Serve immediately.

4 SERVINGS

THE PANCAKES

- 3/4 cup (100 g) buckwheat flour
- 3/4 cup (100 g) wheat flour
- 1 whole egg
- 2 tablespoons warm water
- 5 tablespoons (2 1/2 ounces; 75 g) lightly salted butter
- 3 ounces (90 g) finely-diced fresh truffles

- 20 large langoustines, about 3 ounces (90 g) each
- 2 ounces (6.0 g) goose fat

THE SHELLFISH BOUILLON

- 4 tablespoons (6 cl) extra-virgin olive oil
- 10 ounces (300 g) langoustine heads, rinsed
- 1 tablespoon (15 g) unsalted butter
- 2 small shallots, peeled and chopped
- 1/2 bulb fresh fennel, washed and chopped
- Bouquet garni: several parsley stems, celery leaves, and sprigs of thyme, wrapped in the green part of a leek and securely fastened with a cotton twine
- 1 tablespoon tomato concentrate
- 1 1/4 cups (31 cl) water

THE VEGETABLE GARNISH

- 5 tablespoons (21/2 ounces; 75 g) unsalted butter
- 3 ounces (90 g) celery root, peeled and finely-diced
- Fine sea salt
- Coarse sea salt
- Freshly-ground pepper

Wine suggestion: a Rhône Valley white, such as a splendid Condrieu, original and full-bodied.

Lobster Baked with Truffles and Chestnuts

BY JOËL ROBUCHON

2 SERVINGS

The luting pastry and glaze
- 2 3/4 cups (370 g) unbleached all-purpose flour
- 3 large (100 g) egg whites
- 2 large (100 g) eggs
- A pinch of sugar
- A pinch of salt
- Rosemary
- 1 large egg, for glaze

The chestnuts
- 10 fresh chestnuts in their shells
- 1 quart (1 l) peanut oil for deep frying
- 4 tablespoons (2 ounces; 60 g) unsalted butter
- 6 tablespoons (1 dl) chicken stock
- Bouquet garni: several parsley stems and sprigs of thyme, wrapped in the white part of a leek and securely tied with cotton twine
- Tomato confit from next page
- One 1 pound (500 g) live female lobster

Prepare the luting pastry: in the bowl of an heavy-duty mixer fitted with a dough hook, combine the flour, egg whites whole eggs, sugar, salt and rosemary. Mix at a low speed until blended. Scrape down the sides of the bowl and form the dough into a ball. Cover and set aside to rest for 1 hour. (The resting time will allow the gluten in the flour to relax and make the dough easier to work with.)

Peel the chestnuts: with a small, sharp knife, make a long cut – a tear actually – along both rounded sides of the chestnut, cutting through the tough outer shell and into the brown skin underneath. This will make the chestnut easier to peel. Pour the oil into a heavy metal 2-quart (2 l) saucepan or use a deep-fat fryer. Heat the oil to 320° F (160° C). Fry the chestnuts in batches of 5 or 6 for about 3 minutes, or until the shells curl away from the chestnut meat. Drain thoroughly. When cool, peel, removing and discarding both the tough outer shell and thin brown inner shell.

Preheat the oven to 400° F (200° C; gas mark 6/7). In a large ovenproof skillet, melt 4 tablespoons (2 ounces; 60g) of butter over a moderately high heat. When hot, add the chestnuts and cook, shaking the pan to toss, until the chestnuts are evenly golden but not deep brown and are fork tender, about 15 minutes. Watch carefully, so the chestnuts do not burn. Add the chicken stock and the bouquet garni, and bring to a boil over a high heat. Transfer the skillet with the chestnuts to the oven, and braise, uncovered, until almost all of the liquid has been absorbed, 15 to 20 minutes. Regularly baste the chestnuts with the liquid so they remain moist. Set aside.

Prepare the tomato confit: preheat the oven to the lowest possible setting, about 200° F (80° C; gas mark 1). Arrange the tomato quarters side-by-side on a baking sheet. Sprinkle lightly with salt, pepper and confectioners' sugar.

Scatter the thyme over the tomatoes and place a garlic sliver on top of each quarter. Drizzle with olive oil. Place in the oven and cook until the tomatoes are very soft, about 1 hour. Turn the tomatoes, baste with the juices, and cook until meltingly tender, and reduced to about half their size, about 2 hours total. Check the tomatoes from time to time: They should remain moist and soft. Remove from the oven and allow to cool thoroughly. Set aside.

In a small casserole, bring 2 cups (50 cl) of water to a rolling boil over a high heat. Add 1 tablespoon of salt. Thoroughly rinse the lobster under cold running water. With scissors, cut away the rubberbands or wooden pegs restraining the claws. Holding the body of the lobster with one hand, plunge only the claws into the boiling water. Remove after 30 seconds. Drain. Twist the claw and two articulations off the body of the lobster. Return the claws to the boiling water and simmer for 2 minutes. Remove and drain. Once cooked, gently crack the claw shells with a hammer or a nutcracker, trying not to damage the meat. Extract the meat with a seafood fork: it should come out in a single piece. Set claw meat aside, reserving the shells.

Holding the lobster with both hands, separate the head from the tail. With a long sharp knife, cut the lobster tail crosswise into three equal parts. With a small paring knife, remove the long, thin intestinal tract found in the lower segment of the tail meat. Discard. Set the tail pieces aside. Open the head. Remove and discard the lumpy head sac located near the eyes. Remove and reserve the liver or "tomalley," the brownish liquid found inside the upper area of the head). Remove and reserve the dark green coral that runs parallel to the liver, if present, in the female lobster. Pass the coral and tomalley through a fine-mesh sieve and mix with 3 tablespoons (1 1/2 ounces; 45 g) softened butter. Transfer to a small container, cover securely and refrigerate. Using kitchen scissors, cut the lobster head and shell into pieces for stock. Set aside.

The tomato confit

- 2 roma tomatoes, peeled, cored, seeded and quartered
- Sea salt and black pepper
- A pinch of confectioners' sugar
- 2 sprigs fresh thyme, stemmed
- 4 garlic cloves, slivered
- 2 tablespoons extra-virgin olive oil

The lobster stock

- 2 tablespoons extra-virgin olive oil
- 1 shallot, peeled and sliced
- 1/2 onion, peeled and sliced
- 1/2 carrot, peeled and sliced
- 1/2 branch celery, sliced
- 1/2 bulb fennel, sliced
- 1 whole garlic clove
- 1 star anise
- 1/4 teaspoon fennel seeds
- 1/4 teaspoon black peppercorns
- Bouquet garni: several parsley leaves and sprigs of thyme wrapped in the white part of a leek and securely tied with a cotton twine
- Fine sea salt
- Freshly ground black pepper

● The luting pastry should be well blended. Form it into a ball and set aside to rest for 1 hour.

● Peel the chestnuts. Remove the shell and the thin brown inner skin after the chestnuts are fried and have cooled.

● Braise the chestnuts in a skillet, then in the oven until they are tender.

● Turn the tomatoes half way through cooking and baste with the juices.

● Plunge the lobster, claws first, into boiling water before twisting off the claws and articulations.

● Prepare the lobster stock. Sear the lobster shells until colored.

● Add the vegetables, seasonings and bouquet garni to the stock.

● Strain the stock, pressing down on the shells to extract all flavor. Discard the shells.

Sauce

- 3/4 bulb fennel cut lengthwise into 3 slices
- Sea salt and freshly ground pepper
- Extra-virgin olive oil
- A pinch of saffron
- 1 plump, fresh garlic clove, halved and degermed
- 8 pieces tomato confit
- Curry
- Truffle

Final garnish

- 10 fresh basil leaves
- 1 plump, fresh garlic clove, peeled
- 1 star anise
- 1 branch fresh rosemary

Prepare the lobster stock: in a large saucepan, heat 1 tablespoon olive oil over high heat until it smokes lightly. Add the lobster shells and sear until colored, tossing constantly, 1 to 2 minutes. In another saucepan, heat 1 tablespoon olive oil over moderate heat and sweat the sliced shallot, onion, carrot, celery, fennel, garlic and a pinch of salt, 2 to 3 minutes. Add the vegetables to the lobster shells in the saucepan, and cover 2/3 with water. Add the star anise, fennel seeds, black peppercorns, and the bouquet garni. Cover and simmer for 20 minutes. With a ladle, skim away any impurities that rise to the surface.

Place a fine-mesh sieve in a large bowl. Transfer the lobster pieces and liquid to the sieve, pressing down on the shells to extract the maximum flavor. Discard the shells, reserving the liquid. Prepare the sauce: In a large skillet, heat 2 tablespoons oil until hot but not smoking. Add 3 slices fennel. Lightly salt and pepper the slices, add a pinch of saffron and a halved clove of garlic. Cover and sweat, 2 to 3 minutes without browning.

● Add the tomato confit to the fennel slices and moisten with the lobster stock.

● Pass the sauce through a food mill to extract the maximum of liquid and flavor.

● Season the pieces of lobster tail with salt and pepper. Add a pinch of curry.

● Place the lobster, shell side down , in a skillet with hot oil to give the shells a red color.

Add the tomato confit and the lobster stock. Cover and cook 15 to 20 minutes, until the fennel is cooked. Pass through a food mill to extract the maximum liquid and flavor.

Season the pieces of lobster tail with salt, pepper and curry. In a large skillet, heat 1 tablespoon olive oil until hot but not smoking. Place the portions of lobster shell side down. Do not cook the lobster, but simply heat the shell until it turns slightly red, 1 to 2 minutes. (This step is purely an aesthetic one, so that when the lobster is served, it does not appear undercooked.) Remove the pieces of lobster. Add the minced truffle to the skillet. Add the lobster sauce and bring to a boil.

Preheat the oven (preferably convection) to 475° F (245° C; gas mark 9). (Note: a convection oven will help the luting pastry to brown more evenly). Crack an egg into a small bowl and whisk to blend. Set aside. Place the pieces of lobster in the bottom of a 6 1/2-inch (17 cm) round clear ovenproof (Pyrex) casserole fitted with a lid. Arrange the chestnuts around the lobster. Add the basil, garlic, star anise, and rosemary. Spoon the lobster butter on top of the lobster. Pour the lobster sauce all over. Cut the luting pastry in half and roll each half into a strip 4 inches (10 cm) wide and long enough to wrap halfway around the casserole. Place the lid on the casserole and wrap the dough around the edge, pressing to make a tight seal. With a brush, coat the surface of the pastry with the egg glaze.

Place the casserole in the center of the oven and bake for 12 minutes. Remove from the oven. To serve, break the seal and discard the pastry. Spoon the lobster and other ingredients into two warmed dinner plates, and serve immediately.

LOBSTER BUTTER

Both lobster tomalley and coral can be used to prepare a quick lobster butter. Combine one or both in a blender or a small food processor, and process until smooth with several tablespoons of softened butter. Spread on grilled homemade bread to eat as a snack, or serve alongside a salad.

LUTING A CASSEROLE

Cut the luting pastry in half and roll each half into a strip 4 inches wide and long enough to wrap halfway around the casserole. Place the lid on the casserole and wrap the dough around the edge, pressing to make a tight seal. With a brush, coat the surface of the pastry with the egg glaze.

Wine suggestion: a white Bordeaux, such as a Graves Château de Fieuzal compliments this dish perfectly.

● Sweat the chopped truffle in the skillet, and add the lobster sauce.

● Place the lobster in a clear ovenproof casserole. Add the basil, garlic, star anise and rosemary.

● Add the lobster butter and spoon the lobster sauce all over.

● Wrap the luting dough all round the edge of the casserole to seal in the flavors.

66 THE CHESTNUT IS PERFECT FOR GREETING THE ARRIVAL OF FALL AND ANNOUNCING THE BEGINNING OF HEARTY, WINTRY FARE. 99

SUMMARY

● Joël Robuchon ●

Lobster and chestnuts? Anything is possible with Joël Robuchon, and his "Homard et marrons aux truffes en cocotte lutée" is proof. The combination of flavors – truffles, tomatoes, fresh herbs – serves as the perfect backdrop for the ingenious marriage of earthy chestnuts and sweet lobster, sealed in a casserole to stew in their own juices. Robuchon sets an important example with this dish. Though one might consider grilled or roasted game as the classical foil for chestnuts, Robuchon sends us a different message – a recipe that calls for invention.

● Dominique Bouchet ●

Dominique Bouchet selects pig's foot as the base for his inventive and unusual dish, "Galette de pieds de cochon aux marrons." The pig's foot, slow-cooked with vegetables, is shaped into galettes, cooked until crispy and served with a port sauce and whole sautéed chestnuts. By choosing this method of preparation, Dominique Bouchet has sealed the different elements of his dish into a galette, as if it were a closed casserole. Served with utter simplicity, the dish reflects the direct influence of his master.

•Christophe Cussac•

Christophe Cussac accepts the challenge with an inventive creation. His "Fillet de haddock à la gentiane et brisures de marrons" is a medley of unusual flavors. Combining poached haddock with chestnuts, he adds dimension to the flavor with touches of hazelnut oil, Suze liqueur (an aperitif with a base of yellow gentian, or bitters) and fresh herbs.

•Benoît Guichard•

Benoît Guichard strikes free from the crowd and opts for a dessert. With a sense of complexity and perfection characteristic of his master, Guichard's "Croustillant aux châtaignes et à la gelée de pomme" is a brilliant medley of flavors. Using candied and pureed chestnuts to perfume a simple ice-cream, Guichard tops it with paper-thin chips of apple, crispy wafers lightly perfumed with chocolate, and warmed apple cubes with a hint of lemon and vanilla – simple flavors, but inventively used.

•Philippe Groult•

The "Canette de Challans rôtie a la coriandre et aux marrons" shows off Philippe Groult's capacity for creativity. He roasts a whole duck with a highly perfumed mixture of coriander and honey glaze. The rendered cooking juices are then deglazed with a mixture of vinegar and orange. Each element brings its own delicate perfume to the mix and accentuates the rich flavors of the roast duck. At the last minute, the penetrating flavor of the chestnut is introduced, blending with the woodsy flavor of the girolle mushroom. Each of these ingredients evokes the atmosphere of the forest.

•Maurice Guillouët•

Opting for a more classical combination, Maurice Guillouët's "Pigeon rôti aux marrons grillés au feu de bois" seeks to echo the earthy chestnut with the distinctive flavor of pigeon, by grilling the bird over a wood-burning fire. Touched only with a whisper of onion, the elements create a dish of extreme simplicity, evoking at the same time the themes of the forest and wood smoke flavors.

Galette of Pig's Foot with Chessnuts

BY DOMINIQUE BOUCHET

In a large stockpot, combine the pig's feet, carrot, celery, leek, bouquet garni, garlic and onion. Cover generously with cold water and season with 1 tablespoon salt per quart (liter) of water. Bring to a boil over high heat. Reduce heat to low and simmer 4 to 5 hours skimming any impurities that may rise to the surface. Remove the meat and gelatin from the bones. Discard the bone. Cut or pull the meat and gelatin into small pieces. Discard any hard or very firm portions of meat, gristle, or tendon.

Meanwhile, heat the butter in a small skillet over moderate heat. Add the minced celeriac, cover, and sweat over low heat for 10 minutes.

Place the meat in the bowl of a food processor and pulse on and off until the pork is finely minced. Add half of crushed chestnuts and the celeriac, to the bowl of the processor. Process lightly and season to taste. Transfer to a round mold, measuring 5 inches (12 1/2 cm) in diameter. Cover and refrigerate overnight.

Unmold the pork and cut crosswise into four galettes 1/2-inch (1.25 cm) thick.

Prepare the coating: prepare three shallow bowls. Place the flour in the first bowl. In the second, whisk together the eggs and oil, and season generously. Place the breadcrumbs in the third.

Dip each slice of galette into the flour, turning to coat evenly, and shaking off the excess. Dip into the egg mixture, turning to coat evenly, shaking off the excess. Dip into the bread crumbs, turning to coat evenly, shaking off the excess. Repeat with the remaining galettes.

Prepare the sauce: in a small skillet, reduce the Port until 1 tablespoon remains. Add the demi-glace, stir to blend and taste for seasoning. Set aside and keep warm.

In a large skillet, heat 1 tablespoon of clarified butter over high heat. When it sizzles, add a galette and cook lightly on each side, 1 to 2 minutes. Repeat for the remaining galettes. Lightly warm the whole reserved chestnuts in the remaining tablespoon of butter.

To serve, place a galette in the center of a warmed dinner plate. Arrange six chestnuts around each galette. Spoon the sauce around each galette and serve immediately.

4 SERVINGS

THE PORK BOUILLON

- 4 fresh pig's feet
- 1 small carrot, peeled
- 1 branch celery, washed
- 1 leek, washed, white and tender green parts
- Bouquet garni
- 1/2 head fresh garlic
- 1 onion, peeled
- Sea salt to taste

- 1 tablespoon (15 g) unsalted butter
- 2 ounces (60 g) celeriac, finely minced
- 4 ounces (120 g) grilled chestnuts (reserve 24 chestnuts for garnish; crush the remaining chestnuts lightly)
- Sea salt and freshly ground white pepper to taste

THE COATING

- 1/2 cup (70 g) flour
- 2 large eggs
- 2 tablespoons peanut oil
- 1/2 cup (70 g) fine breadcrumbs
- 5 tablespoons clarified butter

THE SAUCE

- 2 tablespoons red Port wine
- 4 tablespoons demi-glace

Wine suggestion: a Beaujolais, such as a light and racy Fleurie.

Filet of Haddock "Gentiane" with Chestnuts

BY CHRISTOPHE CUSSAC

In a medium-size bowl, combine 2 cups (50 cl) milk and the haddock. Soak for 1 hour. Rinse the fish under cold water, discarding the milk. Set aside.

Preheat the oven to 450° F (230° C; gas mark 9). With a small sharp knife, make a long cut along both rounded sides of the chestnut, cutting through the tough outer shell. Place the chestnuts in a roasting pan with a few tablespoons of water. Place in the center of the oven and roast until the shells curl away from the meat, 3 to 5 minutes. When cool, peel the chestnuts, removing the tough outer shell and thin brown inner skin. Set aside.

Heat a large skillet over a medium heat and lightly brown the bacon. Add the chestnuts and white wine to the skillet. Reduce lightly over moderate heat. Add the chicken stock, 1 carrot, onions, garlic, and bouquet garni and simmer gently over medium heat, 15 minutes. Do not add salt. Remove skillet from the heat and discard the garlic and bouquet garni. Remove the bacon and finely dice. Return to the skillet. Add the remaining carrot. Pour off 4 tablespoons cooking liquid and reserve. Keep the chestnut mixture warm over low heat.

In a saucepan combine the reserved cooking liquid and the lemon juice and bring to a boil over a high heat.
Remove from the heat and whisk in 1 tablespoon of the butter.

Return the pan to low heat, whisking until the butter has melted. Repeat for the remaining 2 tablespoons butter. Stir in the Suze and hazelnut oil. Adjust seasoning. Set aside.

In a large casserole, heat the remaining 2 cups (50 cl) milk over low heat and add the haddock fillets. Simmer gently, 5 to 8 minutes. Set aside.

Add about half the milk used to cook the haddock and the fresh chopped herbs to the chestnuts. Taste for seasoning. Keep warm over a low heat.

Drain the haddock fillets and halve each one.

To serve: spoon the sauce onto four warmed dinner plates. Spoon the chestnut mixture over the sauce. Place a piece of haddock on top. Garnish with parsley leaves. Serve immediately.

4 SERVINGS

- 1 quart (1 l) milk
- 2 haddock fillets, each weighing about 10 ounces (300 g)
- 1 pound (500 g) fresh chestnuts
- 3 ounces (90g) slab bacon, rind removed, halved
- 2 tablespoons white wine
- 2 cups (50 cl) chicken stock
- 2 medium-size carrots, peeled and finely diced
- 2 small onions, peeled and finely diced
- 1 fresh, plump garlic clove, peeled
- Bouquet garni
- 1 tablespoon lemon juice
- 3 tablespoons (45 g) unsalted butter, chilled and cut into pieces
- 1 tablespoon gentiane liqueur (such as Suze)
- 1/2 teaspoon hazelnut oil
- 2 tablespoons finely minced, fresh, flat-leaf parsley leaves
- 1 tablespoon finely mined fresh chervil leaves
- 1 tablespoon finely minced fresh tarragon leaves
- 2 tablespoons finely minced fresh, flat-leaf parsley leaves, for garnish
- Sea salt
- Freshly ground black pepper

Wine suggestion: a white from Provence, such as a fruity Palette with a fine unctuosity.

Roasted Duck
with Coriander and Chestnuts

BY PHILIPPE GROULT

Prepare the honey glaze: in a large saucepan, melt the honey over moderate heat and add the coriander. Add the orange zest and cook, stirring from time to time, for 10 minutes. Remove from the heat to cool completely. Set aside. Preheat the oven to 375° F (185° C; gas mark 4-5).

Prepare the ducks: season the interior of each duck with teaspoon coarse sea salt and truss. In an ovenproof skillet large enough to hold both ducks, combine 1 tablespoon of peanut oil with 6 tablespoons (90 g) butter over moderate heat. Place each duck on its side in the pan and brown lightly over moderate heat. Set the ducks in the oven with the breast portion toward the back. Roast, uncovered, for 10 minutes. Turn the ducks over and roast for 10 minutes more. Spoon the juices over the ducks 3 or 4 times.

Remove from the oven and discard any excess fat. With a ladle, pour the honey-coriander mixture over the ducks. Turn the ducks on their backs and roast for an additional 20 minutes. Remove the ducks from the oven and, once again, season generously. Transfer the ducks to a large platter, reserving the pan and its contents. Place the ducks at an angle against the edge of a baking dish, with their heads down and tail in the air. Cover the ducks loosely with aluminum foil. Turn off the oven and leave the ducks in the oven with the door ajar. Let rest for at least 20 min-utes and up to 1 hour. The ducks will continue to cook.

Prepare the sauce: place the pan with the trimmings over high heat. Add the onion and carrot and cook until nicely browned, 1 to 2 minutes. Deglaze with the vinegar, and add the bay leaf and the orange juice. Cook over moderate heat, 5 to 8 minutes, until well reduced. Strain the sauce thorugh a fine-mesh sieve placed over a clean skillet. Add any cooking juices. Keep warm.

Peel the chestnuts: with a small sharp knife make a long cut along both roundned ends of the chestunt, cutting through the tough outer shell and into the brown skin underneath. This will make the chestnut easier to peel. Heat 3 talbespoons of peanut oil. Fry the chestnuts in batches of 5 or 6 for about 3 minutes, or until the shells curl away from the meat. Peel the chestnuts, removing both the tough outer shell and the thin outer skin. Place the chestnuts in a large saucepan and add the chicken stock. Bring to a boil oer high heat and simmer, uncovered, for 15 to 20 minutes. Take care not to touch them as they cook.

Cook the mushrooms: place the mushrooms in a medium nonstick skillet with no fat added, over moderate heat. Salt, cover, and cook for 3 to 4 minutes. Transfer the mushrooms to a colander and drain the liquid from the skillet. When the mushrooms are cool enough to handle, heat the same skillet over moderate heat. Combine 3 talbespooons (45 g) of butter and the mushrooms and cook until softenend, 3 to 4 minutes. Season to taste. Just before serving, add the tarragon and parsley. Toss to blend. Set aside and keep warm.

To serve: arrange the ducks in the center of a large, warmed platter. Spoon the mushroms and the chestnuts around the ducks. Spoon about half the sauce and the coriander over the ducks. Transfer the rest to a warmed sauceboat. Serve immediately, carving the duck at the table.

4 SERVINGS

- 1 cup (18.5 cl) honey
- 1/4 pound (125 g) whole grains of coriander, lightly crushed
- 2 oranges, zest and juice reserved separately
- 2 ducks, each weighing 3- to 4 pounds (1.8 to 2 kg)
- 4 tablespoons (6 cl) peanut oil
- 9 tablespoons (4 ounces; 135 g) unsalted butter
- 1 large onion, peeled and chopped
- 1 carrot, peeled and chopped
- 4 tablespoons (6 cl) red wine vinegar
- 1 bay leaf
- 20 fresh chestnuts
- 2/3 cup (16 cl) chicken stock
- 2 small shallots, peeled and minced
- 13 ounces (390 g) chanterelle mushrooms
- 1 small bunch fresh tarragon, washed, dried, and finely chopped
- 8 leaves flat-leaf parsley, washed and dried
- Coarse sea salt
- Fine sea salt
- Freshly ground white pepper

Wine suggestion: a red wine from the Rhône valley, such as a Châteauneuf-du-Pape.

Chestnut Ice Cream with apple Chips and Crispy Wafers

BY BENOÎT GUICHARD

Prepare the apple chips: preheat the oven (preferably a convection oven) to 275° F (135° C; gas mark 2). Peel, core, and halve the apples lengthwise. With a mandoline, cut into paper-thin, half-moon slices. Arrange the slices side-by-side on a non-stick baking sheet. Sprinkle both sides with confectioners' sugar. Place the baking sheet in the center of the oven and bake 10 to 12 minutes. Remove from the oven. Once cooled, the apples will turn crispy. Set aside. (You will only need 12 slices for this dessert. The remaining slices can be reserved for a snack.)

Prepare the chestnut ice cream: in a small saucepan combine the cream, milk and glucose bring to a boil over high heat. Remove from the heat and set aside. In the bowl of an electric mixer, whisk the egg yolks with the granulated sugar until thick and lemon-colored. Set aside.

Strain the milk mixture through a fine-mesh sieve into a large saucepan. Bring just to a boil over high heat. Temper one third of the boiling milk/cream mixture into the egg yolk mixture, whisking constantly. Return this milk and egg yolk mixture to the saucepan. Reduce the heat to low and cook, stirring constantly, until the mixture thickens to a creamy consistency. Do not let it boil. When the cream is cooked, add the chestnut puree. Whisk lightly to blend. To test, run your finger down the back of a wooden spoon: if the mixture is sufficiently cooked, the mark will hold. The entire process should take about 5 minutes. Remove the pan from the heat. Pass the mixture through a fine-mesh sieve, and cool completely before placing the mixture in an ice cream maker. (To speed cooling, transfer the cream to a large chilled bowl. Place that bowl inside a slightly larger bowl filled with ice cubes and water. Stir occasionally. To test the temperature, dip your fingers into the mixture: The cream should feel cold to the touch. The process should take about 30 minutes.)

When thoroughly cooled, transfer to an ice cream maker and freeze according to manufacturer's instructions. Five minutes before removing the ice cream from the machine, add the rum and candied chestnuts. Refrigerate.

Prepare the wafers: preheat the oven to 475° F (245° C; gas mark 9). Place a non-stick baking sheet on a work surface. With a 5-inch triangular metal pastry cutter (or substitute a homemade cardboard stencil), make 12 triangles on the sheet by sprinkling the crushed wafers over the stencil. Sprinkle each triangle with a layer of cocoa bean shells and a sprinkling of confectioners' sugar. Place the baking sheet in the center of the oven and bake for 3 minutes. Remove from the oven and allow the triangles to cool on the baking sheet. Set aside.

Prepare the apple garnish: In a medium-size skillet, melt the butter over low heat. Add the diced apples and the vanilla seeds. Saute over medium-high heat until the apples are lightly browned and caramelized, 3 to 4 minutes. Add the lemon juice and the apple jelly and stir to blend. Remove from the heat.

To serve: place a scoop of chestnut ice cream in the center of a plate. Spoon the apple garnish around the ice cream. Decoratively position 3 apple chips and 3 wafers in the ice cream.

Repeat for 3 remaining servings. Serve immediately.

4 SERVINGS

THE APPLE CHIPS

- 1 Granny Smith apple
- 3/4 cup (90 g) confectioners' sugar

THE CHESTNUT ICE CREAM

- 1/2 cup (12.5 cl) heavy cream
- 1 cup (25 cl) whole milk
- 1 tablespoon glucose (optional)
- 3 large egg yolks
- 1/3 cup (65 g) granulated sugar
- 2 1/2 ounces (75 g) chestnut puree
- 1 tablespoon dark rum
- 2 ounces (60 g) candied chestnuts, chopped into small pieces

THE WAFERS

- 2 ounces (60 g) fine wafer cookies from Brittany, crushed
- 1 tablespoon (20 g) finely chopped cocoa bean shells, cooked in a caramel, cooled and chopped into small pieces (optional)

THE APPLE GARNISH

- 2 tablespoons (1 ounce: 30 g) unsalted butter
- 1 Granny Smith apple, peeled, cored, quartered and cut into 1-inch cubes
- 1 plump, moist vanilla bean, split lengthwise, seeds scraped out and reserved
- The juice of 1 lemon, strained
- 3 ounces (90 g) apple jelly

Wine suggestion: a sweet Vouvray from a sunny year, such as 1976.

Broiled Pigeon with Grilled Chestnuts

BY MAURICE GUILLOUËT

In a small saucepan with a tight-fitting lid, combine the onions, the sugar and 2 tablespoons (30 g) butter over moderate heat. Season, add cold water to cover, and cover. Cook until the onions are tender and much of the water has evaporated, 15 to 20 minutes. Keep warm.

Generously season the interior of the pigeons with salt and pepper. Truss. Generously season the outside. Set aside.

Preheat the oven to 500° F (260° C; gas mark 9). (Or prepare a wood or charcoal fire. The fire is ready when the coals glow red and are covered with ash.) In a large ovenproof skillet just large enough to hold the pigeons, melt 1 tablespoon (15 g) butter over high heat. Place the pigeons on their side in the skillet, and set it in the oven with the fullest part of the pigeons (the breast portion) toward the back. Roast, uncovered, for 4 minutes. Turn the pigeons on the other side and roast for 4 minutes more. Turn the pigeons on their back and roast until the juices run clear when a skewer is inserted in the thickest part of the thigh, about 30 minutes total.

Remove the pigeons from the oven, and once again season generously. Transfer the pigeons to a baking dish and place the pigeons at an angle against the edge of the dish, with their heads down and tails in the air. (This heightens the flavor by allowing the juices to flow down through the breast meat.) Set aside. Recuperate the cooking juices and set aside.

Prepare the chestnuts: with a small sharp knife, make a long cut – actually a tear – along both rounded sides of the chestnut, cutting through the tough outer shell and into the brown skin underneath. Place them in a specially designed chestnut skillet with holes and heat the skillet over high heat, tossing constantly, 2 minutes. Place in the center of the oven or over a burner and cook, tossing constantly, 15 to 20 minutes. Remove from the heat and cover the chestnuts loosely with a thick towel. Let them rest for at least 20 minutes. When they are cool, peel the chestnuts, removing both the tough outer shell and the thin brown outer skin. Season with salt and pepper and keep warm.

In a small saucepan, heat the pigeon juices over moderate heat until hot, but not boiling. Set aside.

To serve: carve the pigeons, removing the breast meat and thighs separately. Place the breast meat of each pigeon on a work surface and cut, lengthwise, into 5 or 6 slices. On each warmed dinner plate, place two thighs in the upper area with the slices of breast meat beneath them. Arrange the onions and chestnuts around them. Spoon the cooking juices over the meat. Pour the reserved sauce into a warmed sauceboat. Serve immediately.

4 SERVINGS

- 20 spring onions, peeled
- 1 1/2 tablespoons (20 g) sugar
- 3 tablespoons (1 1/2 ounces; 45 g)
  unsalted butter
- Four 1-pound (500 g) pigeons, wing tips,
  gizzard and heart removed
- 20 unpeeled fresh chestnuts
- Fine sea salt
- Freshly-ground pepper

*Wine suggestion: a red Bordeaux, such as a fine
Pomerol, generous and full-bodied.*

Baby Zucchini with Fresh Almonds

BY JOËL ROBUCHON

4 SERVINGS

INGREDIENTS

- 2 young, baby zucchini (about 6 ounces; 180g) washed but not peeled
- 3 ounces (90 g) fresh, peeled almonds
- 1 tablespoon curry powder
- Sea salt and freshly ground white pepper to taste
- 1 cup (25 cl) peanut oil for frying
- 6 spring onions, peeled and sliced into thin rings
- 1 tablespoon flour
- 6 tablespoons (1 dl) ice cold water
- 4 zucchini blossoms
- 2 1/2 ounces (75 g) lightly smoked bacon, finely diced
- 1 1/2 tablespoons (20 g) unsalted butter
- 1/4 cup (6 cl) extra-virgin olive oil
- 12 mint leaves, cut into a fine julienne

Slice the zucchini into four vertical strips. Remove and discard the pithy interior from each strip. Cut each strip into a 1/4 inch (5 mm) dice.

Place a clean kitchen towel on a flat surface. Place the zucchini, almonds, curry, salt and pepper in the towel and toss to blend. Wrap the towel to cover the ingredients and set aside to rest for 15 minutes. (This will allow the ingredients to absorb the seasoning, making for a more intensely flavored dish.)

Pour the oil into a wide, 3 quart (3 l) saucepan. The oil should be at least 2 inches deep. Place a deep-fry thermometer in the oil and heat the oil to 300 degrees F (150 degrees C).

Place the onion rings in a small colander, toss the onion rounds with the flour, shake off any excess, and fry until golden, about 3 minutes. With a wire skimmer, lift the onions from the oil, drain, and transfer to paper towels. Immediately season with sea salt. Set aside.

Prepare the zucchini blossom batter: In a small bowl, combine the flour and ice water. Set aside.

Reheat the oil to 300 °F (150 °C).

Cut each zucchini blossom vertically into thirds. With tongs or your fingers, dip each section of the blossom into the batter, rolling to coat evenly. Shake off any excess batter, letting it drip back into the bowl. Carefully lower the blossoms, a few at a time, into the oil.

Fry until golden on all sides, turning once, for a total cooking time of about 2 minutes. With a wire skimmer, lift the blossoms from the oil, drain, and transfer to paper towels. Immediately season each side of each leaf with sea salt. Set aside.

● Zucchini blossoms, baby zucchini, and fresh almonds.

● Cut the zucchini into 1/4-inch (5mm) dice.

● Slice the onions into thin rings.

● Combine the zucchini, almonds, pepper, salt and curry.

● Toss the onion rings in the flour, shaking off any excess.

● Remove the fried onion rings with a skimmer when golden, after about 3 minutes of cooking.

● Drain the onion rings on paper towels.

● Carefully lower the zucchini blossoms coated with batter into the hot oil.

In a small skillet, combine the bacon and butter over moderate heat and sauté just until lightly browned, about 3 minutes. Drain and set aside.

In a small skillet, heat the oil over moderately high heat until hot but not smoking. Add the almond and zucchini mixture and sauté for 3 to 4 minutes. The zucchini should remain slightly crunchy.

● When the zucchini blossoms are golden on one side, turn them.

● Remove the fried zucchini blossoms with a wire skimmer and drain on paper towels.

● Brown the bacon, stirring with a wooden spatula.

● Cut the mint leaves in fine julienne.

Add the mint, toss, and taste for seasoning, adding another pinch of curry powder, if desired. Drain and set aside.

To serve: place a small dome of the zucchini mixture in the center of each plate. Sprinkle with bacon, the zucchini flowers and fried onion. Serve immediately.

Wine suggestion: a Savennières, a flagship from the slopes of the Loire.

● Sauté the almond and zucchini mixture for 3 to 4 minutes.

● At the end of the cooking, add the mint and taste for seasoning.

● Place a spoonful of the zucchini mixture in the center of a serving plate.

● Garnish with the bacon, onions, and the pieces of zucchini blossoms.

❝ IN SELECTING FRESH ALMONDS AS ONE OF HIS ESSENTIAL INGREDIENTS, JOËL ROBUCHON CHALLENGES HIS STUDENTS TO CREATE A DISH THAT IS TOTALLY MODERN, A DISH THAT MUST TAKE INTO ACCOUNT THE SWEET, THE DELICATE, THE ELEGANT, ALMOST INTANGIBLE ELEMENT OF THE FRUIT. **❞**

SUMMARY

●

● Joël Robuchon ●

With his "Etuvée de jeunes courgettes aux amandes fraîches, lardons et menthe," Joël Robuchon creates an innovative dish which demonstrates the astute comprehension of lightness that characterizes modern cooking. He blends fresh almonds and zucchini with a touch of curry, his favorite seasoning after salt. He rounds out the dish by adding fresh mint and fried zucchini flower to awaken the palate and the senses.

● Dominique Bouchet ●

Dominique Bouchet rises to the occasion with his "Filet de bar aux pistaches et amandes blanches." Responding with the same emphasis to lightness, Bouchet tops a morsel of steamed sea bass with a layer of almond and pistachio slivers. Dressed on a bed of fresh spinach with a sauce perfumed with mussel juices, tomatoes and shallots, the garnish, like Robuchon's fresh mint, lightens the combination of fish and nuts. Yet the complexity of the dish thoroughly reflects the influence of the Robuchon kitchen.

• Christophe Cussac •

Christophe Cussac's "Gelée de saumon de fontaine en civet aux crevettes et amandes fraîches" combines layers of salmon and shrimp, vegetables and almonds. As one samples the dish, each flavor reveals another – just as the mint and the almonds emerge slowly in Joël Robuchon's zucchini – creating a complex interplay between sweet vegetables and the salt of the sea.

• Benoît Guichard •

The "Dos de Saint-Pierre rôti aux amandes et to-mates confites" injects lightness, spiritedness, acidity and a welcome touch of regionalism to a simple fillet of John Dory. Bathed with a boldly acidic confit of tomatoes, tender baby onions, pungent garlic, forward-flavored fresh thyme and the sweet almonds, this dish all but cries out to be served at a long, languid meal on a summer's day in Provence.

• Philippe Groult •

Philippe Groult also looks back into the classics with a dish that recalls the pairing of asparagus and hollandaise sauce. Groult lightens his "Asperges vertes à l'émulsion d'amandes douces" with whispers of radish, almonds, and marjoram – flavors that add both sweetness and acidity to the equation.

• Maurice Guillouët •

Maurice Guillouët also creates a dish with an emphasis on lightness, taking his inspiration from the classic "trout with almonds." Guillouët's "Sole meunière aux amandes fraîches et salicornes," pairs the smooth texture of fresh almonds with crispy "green beans of the sea" – a texture that echoes the delicate crispness of Robuchon's zucchini flowers. The result is a simple, rustic dish.

Sea Bass with Pistachios and White Almonds

BY DOMINIQUE BOUCHET

Prepare the fish: place the fillets on a plate. With a brush, coat the fillets generously with the softened butter. Season generously with salt and pepper. In a small bowl, toss together the two nuts to blend evenly. Spoon an even layer of nuts on top of the buttered fish. Set aside.

Prepare the sauce: In a medium-size saucepan, combine the mussel liquid, wine, and shallot. Season lightly with salt and pepper. Bring to a boil over moderately-high heat and reduce to about 2 tablespoons. Remove the saucepan from the heat and whisk in 2 tablespoons of the cold butter. Return the pan to low heat, whisking until the butter has melted. Remove the saucepan from the heat and whisk in 2 more tablespoons butter. Add the remaining 2 tablespoons butter, whisking until blended. Taste for seasoning. Never allow the sauce to boil. (If a smooth sauce is desired, strain through a fine-mesh seive to remove the shallots.) Keep warm, uncovered, in the top of a double boiler over gently simmering water.

Bring 1 quart (1 l) water to a simmer in the bottom of a steamer. Place the fillets, dressed side up, on the steaming rack. Place the rack over the simmering water, cover, and steam until the fillets are opaque through, 4 to 5 minutes for medium-rare, 6 to 8 minutes for medium.

Meanwhile, in a skillet, heat the remaining 2 tablespoons butter over moderate heat until the butter sizzles. Add the spinach leaves and cook, 1 minute, tossing constantly.

To serve: arrange a mound of spinach leaves in the center of each of four warmed dinner plates. Flatten the spinach out to form a small "galette." Place the fillet on top of the spinach.

Add the tomatoes and chives to the sauce and whisk to blend. Drizzle the sauce all around the edges of the plate. Repeat for the remaining three servings. Transfer the remaining sauce to a warmed sauceboat. Serve immediately.

4 SERVINGS

THE FISH

- 4 sea bass fillets, skinned, each weighing
  5 ounces (150 g)
- 4 tablespoons (2 ounces; 60 g) unsalted butter,
  softened
- Sea salt and freshly ground white pepper
  to taste
- 4 tablespoons skinned pistachios,
  finely chopped
- 4 tablespoons skinned white almonds,
  finely chopped

THE SAUCE

- 1 tablespoon cooking liquid from mussels
- 2 tablespoons white wine
- 1 small shallot, peeled and minced
- 6 tablespoons (3 ounces; 90 g) unsalted butter,
  chilled
- 2 tomatoes, peeled, cored, seeded and chopped
- 1 tablespoon very finely minced fresh chives

THE SPINACH GARNISH

- 3 ounces (90 g) spinach leaves, stemmed,
  washed and dried
- 2 tablespoons (1 ounce; 30 g) unsalted butter

*Wine suggestion: a white from Provence, such as
a Palette.*

Gelee of Salmon with Shrimp and fresh Almonds

BY CHRISTOPHE CUSSAC

Place onion, salt, vinegar, and peppercorns in small container. Cover, store at room temperature 2 months. Cut into matchsticks.

Prepare the lemon confit: in a small bowl, toss salt, sugar and lemons. Cover, store at room temperature 3 weeks, tossing from time to time. Trim skin from lemons and julienne.

Place the wine in a large saucepan and reduce over high heat, 3 to 5 minutes. Add the gray shrimp and simmer for 20 minutes. Strain, reserving the broth.

Place gelatin in small bowl of water. Bloom for 10 minutes. Squeeze out excess water.

In a small saucepan, bring 1/2 cup (12.5 cl) water to boil over a high heat. Add gelatin and stir to dissolve.

Add bouillon. Bring to a boil. Taste for seasoning. Set aside. Cut salmon into thin slices, season, and line molds with the fish. Reserve the scraps, dice, and steam 3 to 4 minutes. Refrigerate.

When gelatin begins to set, pour a little in the bottom of each mold and arrange 2 red shrimp halves on top. Refrigerate. Add half the vegetables, chopped almonds, and fish scraps. Pour gelatin to the top. Refrigerate.

In small bowl, fold the lemon juice into the whipped cream. Taste for seasoning. Set aside. Remove molds from the salmon and turn onto baking sheet. Baste with gelatin that has not fully set. Refrigerate. Repeat several times to achieve an even coating.

In a small bowl, whisk vinegar and salt. Add 4 teaspoons of olive oil, whisking to blended. Season with pepper. Pour over mesclun, add remaining vegetables and bacon, and toss. In a small bowl, toss 4 teaspoons olive oil with whole almonds and red onions.

Arrange salad on one side of each of four dinner plates. Place salmon alongside. Place dollop of cream alongside. Sprinkle cream with lemon chervil and chives.

Place a mound of almond mixture alongside. Serve.

4 SERVINGS

THE RED ONION CONDIMENT

- 1 medium-size red onion, peeled, sliced,
  blanched and refreshed
- 1 tablespoon (15 g) table salt
- 2 cups (50 cl) white vinegar
- 1 tablespoon whole peppercorns

THE LEMON CONFIT

- 1/2 cup (100 g) sea salt
- 1 teaspoon sugar
- 4 lemons, washed and quartered lengthwise
  When ready, remove the skin from 1 quarter
  of a lemon and cut into a fine julienne
- Bouillon
- 5 1/2 sheets gelatin
- 2 salmon fillets, each about 12 ounces (375g),
  deboned with the skin intact
- 4 red shrimp, cooked and halved
- 2 medium-size carrots, peeled, diced, blanched
  and refreshed
- 2 medium-size zucchini, diced, blanched
  and refreshed
- 3 ounces (100 g) whole peeled almonds,
  12 reserved whole, the rest finely chopped
- 1 tablespoon lemon juice
- 4 tablespoons heavy cream, whipped
- 1 teaspoon sherry vinegar
- Salt and fresh ground pepper
- 8 teaspoons olive oil
- 2 ounces (60 g) mesclun (mixed baby greens)
- 4 thin slices lightly smoked bacon, broiled
  and minced
- Juice of 1/2 lemon
- 2 tablespoons chervil, stemmed, washed,
  and finely chopped
- 2 tablespoons minced chives

SPECIAL MATERIAL

- 4 small baking tins, 3 inches (7.5 cm) wide,
  1 inch (2.5 cm) deep

*Wine suggestion: a delicately perfumed red Givry
from Burgundy.*

Asparagus with Hollandaise and Fresh Almonds

BY PHILIPPE GROULT

Prepare the asparagus: place each asparagus on a flat work surface. Trim the bottom of each on a diagonal for presentation. With a vegetable peeler, begin at the tip and peel evenly down to the bottom of each asparagus. Peel all around each one evenly, removing the tough outer skin. All asparagus should all be the same size.

Cook the asparagus: prepare a large bowl of ice water. Bring a large pot of water to a boil over high heat. Add salt and the asparagus. Cover and cook until tender when pierced with a knife, about 15 minutes. Drain, shock in ice water and drain again. Set aside.

Prepare the hollandaise: in a small bowl, whisk together the egg yolks and water until smooth. Transfer the mixture to the top of a double boiler. (The top container should not touch the water or the mixture will heat too quickly. Do not cover the pan or drops of water will drip into the hollandaise and alter its texture.) Cook, whisking constantly, until the eggs form ribbons and the mixture doubles in volume. Gradually add just a few drops of the clarified butter at a time while whisking continuously until thoroughly incorporated. Do not add too much butter at the beginning or the mixture will not emulsify. As soon as the mixture begins to thicken, add the remaining butter, slowly and steadily, whisking constantly. Add the lemon juice and the cream and whisk to blend. Season lightly with salt and cayenne pepper. Set aside and keep warm.

When the asparagus are cooked, arrange them in a single layer on a clean towel. With a brush, gently coat them with olive oil and sprinkle lightly with paprika. Set aside. Sprinkle the radish slices with paprika as well. Set aside.

To serve, spoon the hollandaise in the center of four warmed dinner plates. Arrange 3 asparagus side by side, then cross with 2 additional asparagus. Sprinkle with radish slices and almonds. Spoon more sauce over the vegetables.

Garnish with marjoram and serve immediately, passing a sauceboat of hollandaise.

4 SERVINGS

- 20 large asparagus spears, trimmed

THE HOLLANDAISE

- 4 large egg yolks
- 1 tablespoon cold water
- 12 tablespoons (6 ounces; 180 g)
  clarified butter
- Juice of half a lemon
- 1 teaspoon heavy cream
- Cayenne pepper

- 1 teaspoon extra-virgin olive oil
- Paprika
- 5 small radishes, washed and thinly sliced
- 2 ounces (60 g) fresh whole almonds, peeled
- 1 tablespoon fresh marjoram, stemmed
  and washed
- Fine sea salt

*Wine suggestion: a wine from the Herault region
of France, preferably a chardonnay.*

Whole Roasted John Dory
with Almonds and Tomato Confit

BY BENOÎT GUICHARD

Prepare the tomato confit: preheat the oven to the lowest possible setting, about 200° F (80° C; gas mark 1). Arrange the tomato quarters side-by-side on a baking sheet. Sprinkle each side lightly with salt, pepper and confectioners' sugar. Scatter the thyme leaves over the tomatoes and place a garlic sliver on top of each quarter. Drizzle with olive oil. Place in the oven and cook until the tomatoes are very soft, about 1 hour. Turn the tomatoes, baste with the juices, and cook until meltingly tender, and reduced to about half their size, about 2 hours total. Check the tomatoes from time to time: they should remain moist and soft. Remove from the oven and allow to cool thoroughly. Set aside.

Prepare the vegetable/fish fumet: in a large saucepan, combine the shallots, leek, fennel, salt, and oil. Sweat over medium heat until soft, 3 to 5 minutes. Add the celery and star anise. Season the fish head (or extra bones) with salt and pepper and add to the pan. Add 2/3 cup (16 cl) water, the dry vermouth, and the white wine, and simmer, about 5 minutes. Cover and cook over moderate heat, about 15 minutes. Pass through a fine-mesh sieve, discarding the solids. Set aside.

Prepare the lemon sections: cut both ends off 1 lemon. Place the lemon, cut end down, on a work surface. With a small, sharp knife, cutting downward, slice off a strip of peel, following the curve of the lemon. Continue cutting away strips of peel with the pith until it is completely removed. To separate and lift out each lemon section, begin by slicing between the membrane and the fruit of each section, and carefully lift it out. Move to the next lemon section, and slice between the membrane and the fruit. Continue with the other lemon until all of the sections have been removed. In a small bowl, reserve the sections. Set aside.

Preheat the oven to 350° F (175° C; gas mark 4/5). Season the fish inside and out with salt and pepper. Drizzle 3 tablespoons of oil over the bottom of an oval roasting pan or white porcelain baking dish large enough to generously hold the fish. Place the fish in the center. Arrange around the sides of the fish the halved onions, garlic, lemon sections, and almonds. Roll each piece of confit of tomato and arrange around the fish. Place the parsley leaves on top of the vegetable garnish. Season with thyme and pepper. Cut the butter into cubes and in the thickest area of the fish.

Place the fish in the center of the oven and roast for 10 minutes. Remove from the oven and baste. Turn the onions, so they cook evenly. Pour the fish stock around the vegetable garnish. Return to the oven and roast 3 to 5 additional minutes.

Remove from the oven. With a small knife, gently lift away the flesh from the thickest area of the fillet. The meat should be firm and white, and lift easily off the bone. If the flesh sticks or is light pink or translucent, cook 3 to 4 minutes more, for a total of about 20 minutes.

Remove the fish from the oven and serve in its baking dish. The fish can be filleted at the table, transferring each portion of fish and the garnish to a prewarmed dinner plate.

4 SERVINGS

THE TOMATO CONFIT

- 4 roma tomatoes, peeled, cored, seeded
  and quartered
- Sea salt and freshly ground black pepper
- Confectioners' sugar
- 2 sprigs fresh thyme, stemmed
- 4 plump, fresh garlic cloves, peeled, slivered
- 2 tablespoons extra-virgin olive oil

THE VEGETABLE/FISH FUMET

- 2 shallots, peeled and minced
- 1 leek, cleaned and minced
- 1 small bulb fennel, trimmed and minced
- Sea salt to taste
- 2 tablespoons extra-virgin olive oil
- 1 branch celery, minced
- 1 star anise, broken into bits
- 1/4 cup (6 cl) dry vermouth (Noilly-Prat)
- 1/4 cup (6 cl) dry white wine

- 1 whole John Dory (about 3 pounds; 1.5 kg),
  or substitute red snapper or porgy, cleaned,
  with spines removed and discarded
  Reserve the head and refrigerate.
  (Or ask your fishmonger to do this for you.)

THE ROASTING GARNISH

- 2 lemons
- 8 spring onions, peeled and halved lengthwise
- 4 plump, fresh garlic cloves, peeled and halved
- 3 ounces (90 g) fresh peeled almonds
  (or substitute blanched whole almonds)
- 40 leaves flat-leaf parsley
- 8 sprigs fresh thyme
- 5 tablespoons (2 1/2 ounces; 75 g)
  unsalted butter

*Wine suggestion: a dry and generous white, such
as Chassagne-Montrachet, white Burgundy.*

Sole Meunière with Fresh Almonds and Salicornes

BY MAURICE GUILLOUËT

Prepare the salicornes: prepare a large bowl of ice water. Bring a large pot of water to a rolling boil. Add 1 tablespoon salt per quart of water, and add the salicornes. Cook for 2 minutes. Remove with a slotted spoon and transfer to the ice water. Once cooled, drain and set aside.

Prepare the almonds: in a medium-size skillet, heat 2 tablespoons (30 g) butter. Add the almonds and toss to coat the almonds. Cook over moderate heat, 4 to 5 minutes. Drain and taste for seasoning. Keep warm.

In a small skillet, combine the salicornes with 2 tablespoons butter (30 g) and the water over moderate heat. Heat just to warm through, stirring gently, 2 to 3 minutes. Taste for seasoning.

Cook the soles: season the soles with salt and pepper. In a large nonstick skillet, heat the oil and 3 tablespoons (45 g) butter over moderately high heat. When hot, add the soles, skinless side down, in the skillet. Cook without turning until the underside is lightly browned, 2 to 3 minutes. With a wide spatula, turn the soles over and cook for an additional 2 to 3 minutes. Leave the soles in the pan and remove them from the heat. The soles will continue to cook as you dress the plates.

To finish: heat a small saucepan over high heat until hot, but not smoking. Add the remaining butter and wait for it to brown slightly. Add the lemon juice. Dress the sole on warmed plates. Spoon the salicornes and the almonds around them. Add the chives to the butter and spoon it over the fish. Serve immediately.

4 SERVINGS

- 3 ounces (90 g) fresh salicornes
- 10 tablespoons (5 ounces; 150 g) unsalted butter
- 10 ounces (300 g) fresh almonds, shelled
- 2 tablespoons water
- 1 tablespoon peanut oil
- 4 fresh soles (10 to 12 ounces; 300 - 350 g each), gutted, heads and black skin removed
- Juice of 1 lemon
- 2 tablespoons minced chives

Wine suggestion: a Burgundy, such as a white Rully.

PREPARATION AND COOKING TIMES

• POTATOES •

• Potato puree
Joël Robuchon . . . . .2 h
• Potatoes sautéed in butter with thyme
Dominique Bouchet .2 h 15
• Potato puree with Chaource cheese
Christophe Cussac . . . . .1 h
• Brandade of baby red mullet
Philippe Groult . . . . .5 h
• Individual potato gratins
Benoît Guichard . . . . .1 h 45
• Fricassée of lobster with potatoes
Maurice Guillouët . . . . .2 h

• CAVIAR •

• Lobster aspic and caviar with cauliflower cream
Joël Robuchon . . . . .6 h 30
• Potato tart with smoked salmon and caviar
Dominique Bouchet . . . . .45 mn
• Egg cups of lobster with quail eggs and caviar
Christophe Cussac . . . . .1 h 35
• Spider crab with caviar served in the shell
Philippe Groult . . . . .2 h 45
• Apple, caviar, and red onion salad
Benoît Guichard .1 h 20
• Cannelloni of sea trout with caviar
Maurice Guillouët . . . . .1 h 15

• SCALLOPS •

• Scallops roasted in their shells with herbs and butter
Joël Robuchon . . . . .3 h 30
• Scallop quenelles on a bed of mushroom puree
Dominique Bouchet . . . . .1 h 45
• Scallops with lemon confit and potato chips
Christophe Cussac . . . . .3 h 30
• Skewers of scallops and smoked eel
Philippe Groult . . . . .2 h
• Grilled scallops with warm fennel salad
Benoît Guichard .3 h 30
• Scallop ravioli with vegetable butter
Maurice Guillouët . . . . .2 h 30

• CÈPES •

• Grilled wild mushrooms with thyme and eggplant caviar
Joël Robuchon . . . . .3 h 30
• Cèpe terrine with scrambled eggs
Dominique Bouchet . . . . .1 h 45
• Roasted monkfish with smoked salt and cèpes
Christophe Cussac . . . . .1 h 15
• Sautéed cèpes with Serano ham
Philippe Groult . . . . .1 h 45
• Wild mushroom and duck confit tarts
Benoît Guichard .3 h 30
• Sliced cèpes with abalone
Maurice Guillouët . . . . .1 h 30

● SWEETBREADS ●

● Truffled sweetbreads with romaine lettuce
and herbal cream sauce
Joël Robuchon . . . . .6 h
● Salad of sweetbreads and asparagus
Dominique Bouchet .1 h 45
● Sweetbreads with fava beans and summer savory
Christophe Cussac . . . . .3 h 30
● Whole sweetbreads with cabbage and nuts
Philippe Groult . . . . .1 h
● Sweetbreads with morels and new baby onions
Benoît Guichard . . . . .1 h 30
● Sweetbreads with artichokes
and Jesuralem artichoke chips
Maurice Guillouët . . . . .1 h 30

● TRUFFLES ●

● Truffle, onion, and bacon tartlets
Joël Robuchon . . . . .4 h 30
● Brandade of fresh cod with white truffles
Dominique Bouchet .1 h 15
● Pot-au-feu with foie gras and "countryman's" truffles
Christophe Cussac . . . . .4 h 30
● Aspic and foie gras with truffles
Philippe Groult . . . . .4 h
● Cannelloni with fresh truffles
Benoît Guichard . . . . .2 h
● Crispy pancakes and langoustines with truffles
Maurice Guillouët . . . . .2 h 15

● CHESTNUTS ●

● Lobster baked with truffles and chestnuts
Joël Robuchon . . . . .10 h
● Galette of pig's foot with chestnuts
Dominique Bouchet . . . . .7 h
● Fillet of haddock "gentiane" with chestnuts . . . .
Christophe Cussac . . . . .3 h 30
● Roasted duck with coriander and chestnuts
Philippe Groult . . . . .2 h
● Chestnut ice cream with apple chips and crispy wafers
Benoît Guichard . . . . .2 h
● Broiled pigeon with grilled chestnuts
Maurice Guillouët . . . . .2 h 15

● ALMONDS ●

● Baby zucchini with bacon, fresh almonds and mint
Joël Robuchon . . . . .4 h 30
● Sea bass with pistachios and white almonds
Dominique Bouchet .1 h 15
● Gelée of "fontaine" salmon with shrimp
and fresh almonds
Christophe Cussac . . . . .4 h
● Asparagus with Hollandaise and fresh almonds
Philippe Groult . . . . .1 h 30
● Whole roasted John Dory with almonds and tomato confit
Benoît Guichard . . . . .3 h 30
● Sole meunière with fresh almonds and salicornes
Maurice Guillouët . . . . .1 h 15

LIST OF RECIPES

Acknowledgments

• **Hachette Pratique** would especially like to thank Sylvie Girard for her part in the realization of this book.

• **Patricia Wells** would like to thank Alexandra Guarnaschelli for her invaluable help in the writing and proof-reading of the text.

• **Hervé Amiard** would like to thank the firms Kodak France, Nikon France and Rush Labo in Paris, as well as the entire staff of Joel Robuchon's restaurant for their kindness and patience, and in particular Joël Robuchon for the trust he displayed during the years at 59, Avenue Raymond-Poincaré.

• **Laurence Mouton** would like to thank Michel Bernardaud and also La Vaisselle Blanche for their precious support.

———————————————— ● ————————————————

Where to find Joël Robuchon's students:

● **Dominique Bouchet**
Le Moulin de Marcouze - 17 240 Mosnac.
Tél. : 05 46 70 46 16 - Fax : 05 46 70 48 14

● **Christophe Cussac**
L'Abbaye Saint-Michel - 89 700 Tonnerre.
Tél. : 03 86 55 05 99 - Fax 03 86 55 00 10

● **Phillippe Groult**
L'Amphyclès - 78, avenue des Ternes 75017 Paris.
Tél. : 0140 68 01 01 - Fax : 01 40 68 91 88

● **Maurice Guillouët**
Château Taillevent-Robuchon - Tokyo Japon.
Tél. : 03 54 24 13 38 - Fax 81 35 42 41 342

● **Benoît Guichard**
Restaurant Jamin 32, rue de Longchamp 75016 Paris.
Tél. : 01 47 53 00 07

ACHEVÉ D'IMPRIMER EN ITALIE
PAR ROTOLITO LOMBARDA
3002012311720/01
DÉPÔT LÉGAL: 3401 - 08-1997
N° D'EDITION: 41877